NATURE'S WILD HARVEST

NATURE'S WILD HARVEST

Eric Soothill
& Michael J. Thomas

BLANDFORD

This edition first published in the UK 1990 by
Blandford
An imprint of Cassell
Villiers House, 41/47 Strand, London WC2N 5JE

Copyright © 1983 and 1990 Blandford Press

Distributed in the United States by
Sterling Publishing Co. Inc.
387 Park Avenue South, New York, NY 10016.

Distributed in Australia by
Capricorn Link (Australia) Pty Ltd
PO Box 665, Lane Cove, NSW 2066

British Library Cataloguing in Publication Data
Soothill, Eric
  Nature's wild harvest. – 2nd ed.
  1. Food: Wild fruit dishes – Recipes   2. Food: Wild
  vegetable dishes – Recipes
  I. Title   II. Thomas, Michael J. (Michael John), 1952 –
  641.64

    ISBN 0-7137-2226-6

Design by Peter Luff
Photographs by Eric Soothill and Michael J. Thomas
Drawings by Vanessa Luff

Phototypeset by Oliver Burridge & Co. Ltd

Printed in Singapore by
Toppan Printing Co. (S) Ltd.

Contents

Introduction

There is no doubt that we live in the age of the 'tin-can' diet, unaware of the vast store of food available from our countryside. It is surprising to think that we are prepared to pay ever-increasing prices for processed food, neglecting the fact that our wild harvest is free and there to be gathered. All the goodness is retained in the natural food of the wild, which is something that cannot be said of most processed foods nowadays. It may be that our generation has decided that gathering nature's harvest is a timewasting exercise for little reward. Nothing could be further from the truth, even if we only consider the great enjoyment of wandering the countryside or seashore in search of the free pickings. With experience, good gathering-places will be found, which can then be harvested in future years.

People have reverted to making use of wild food only in times of food shortages. During the Second World War, for example, tons of nettles were gathered for use as green vegetables; hawthorn berries or 'haws' and rowanberries were both used to make preserves, and vast quantities of rosehips were collected and turned into a vitamin C rich syrup. Shortages during the war are rapidly being forgotten; surely we do not have to suffer similar disasters before we realize the wealth of food still available around us.

More than 300 plants have been described as edible in Britain. Admittedly, some of these are worthless as food, but many are excellent if prepared correctly; however, we make little use of them. We lag behind the Europeans in this respect, where a considerable trade exists in the wild harvest. For example, the French markets offer a range of edible fungi, and in large quantities. Many of these are far superior in taste to our cultivated mushrooms. Most of us are unaware of the fact that the mushrooms we consume when we eat dried or tinned soups are not those that we are accustomed to buying in the shops; but we cannot deny the superb flavour that these soups have. In fact there are over 50 good edible species of fungi growing in Britain and, contrary to popular belief, few species are deadly poisonous.

One of the richest sources of free food is the seashore. Shellfish are rich in protein and minerals and seaweed is a particularly nutritious food containing a wide variety of important elements and vitamins. Eating seaweed tends to be localized; laver is a traditional food in South Wales and North Devon whereas dulse and carragheen are eaten in parts of Scotland and Ireland. However, some caution is necessary when gathering from the shore: where there is a possibility of pollution from sewerage outlets or large industries, the area should be avoided.

This book covers most of the common wild foods found in Britain. The time of year they are likely to be at their best is indicated, but of course considerable overlap can occur from one month to another. All species are illustrated to aid identification, but although some plants may be shown to be in flower, this does not necessarily mean that they should be used in this state. The descriptive text, line drawings and photographs should adequately help to identify any particular specimen; if some doubt exists, it should be left alone or an authority on the subject should be consulted.

There are numerous recipes recommended within the text; these have been found to be successful in the past. Since wine-making, jam-making and jelly-making recipes predominate, a fuller account of these processes is included in the introduction.

Care has been taken to omit any plant threatened with extinction, and those plants which, if removed from our hedgerows, would severely impair the beauty of the countryside: examples of these are primroses and cowslips, both of which make excellent wines. Some of the plants included are only locally common and therefore gathering from places where they are not plentiful should be discouraged. Also, when wild food is harvested, care should be taken not to strip any single plant of all its leaves, berries or flowers. Avoid gathering near busy roads where pollution from traffic will inevitably find its way onto the roadside plants.

Finally, it is hoped that many enjoyable hours will be spent searching for, gathering and eating the wild harvest. Nevertheless, please remember to obey the code of the countryside at all times.

Jam- and Jelly-making

A wide variety of delicious jams and jellies can be made from nature's wild harvest. Jam and jelly made from plentiful free fruit not only makes good economic sense but also it possesses a luxurious wholesome flavour which bears no comparison with those commercially produced. Large quantities can be made and stored for the year at very little cost. To be successful in jam-making, certain rules need to be observed carefully; these rules, together with the equipment required, are set out below.

Useful Equipment

Preserving pan This is the most important item and should be made from either aluminium or copper. The former is probably better, as it is cheaper to buy and can also be used for making chutneys (the vinegar in chutneys would react with the copper). The pan is wider across the top than the bottom to allow rapid evaporation, and deep for quick boiling once the sugar has been added.

Glass jam jars These should be clean and free of cracks, and can be used over and over again.

Wooden spoon Buy one with a long handle and keep it just for jams and jellies.

Cellophane jam covers, waxed circles, rubber bands and labels Packets containing all four can be purchased from chemists and hardware stores.

Jam funnel This enables the jars to be filled easily without any possibility of scalding.

Jelly-bag This is needed to strain the juice for jelly-making, and can be bought ready-made. However it can be made quite easily from a square 20 × 20 inches (50 × 50 cm) of flannel or calico. Make it into a triangle and sew the seam firmly by machine ensuring that the tip is well joined. Sew on four pieces of tape to the top at equal intervals.

Jelly stand Not a vital piece of equipment, but it is a help when using a jelly-bag. A temporary make-do stand can be made by turning a stool upside down. Fasten the four corners of the jelly-bag to the legs of the stool and place a bowl underneath.

Cooking thermometer Using a cooking thermometer is an accurate way to test for setting. When the thermometer shows a temperature of 220°F (105°C), the setting point has normally been reached.

Basic Steps to Successful Jam-Making

1 Pick dry, firm, ripe fruit.

2 Wash the fruit and place in a preserving pan. An easy method of washing soft fruit is to place in a sieve and immerse in cold water several times.

3 Stew the fruit slowly to extract pectin (the natural setting substance) and to soften the skins of the fruit. To achieve a good set there must be the correct proportions of pectin, acid and sugar. The release of pectin is speeded up by the acid and reacts with the sugar to form a gel. Some fruits, e.g. raspberries, only have small quantities of pectin, but setting can be achieved by adding the juice of apples, redcurrants or lemons; sometimes commercially-prepared pectin can be used.

4 Warm the sugar in the oven before adding to the fruit as this will make it dissolve more quickly, thus shortening the cooking time and improving the colour and set. Stir until the sugar is completely dissolved to ensure that the jam does not burn.

5 When the sugar has dissolved, boil rapidly without stirring.

6 Test for setting by putting a little jam on a cold china saucer, allow it to cool and then run a finger through it. If the jam crinkles slightly it is ready for potting. Remember when testing the jam to remove the preserving pan from the heat. Test the jam early because if boiled too long it may not set and the colour and flavour of the jam may also be spoilt.

7 Skim the scum off the top of the jam if necessary, or if there is not much scum stir it into the jam.

8 If the jam does not contain whole fruit, pour it immediately into warm, clean, dry jamjars. If the jam does contain whole fruit, leave the pan to stand for 30 minutes on a cold surface, then stir before pouring, to avoid the fruit rising in the jars. Fill each jar to the brim to allow for shrinkage, then immediately place a waxed circle, with the waxed surface downwards, on the top of each jar and press slightly to release any air bubbles. Moisten one side of the cellophane cover, place wet side up on the jar and secure with a rubber band: the cellophane contracts to a tight fit as it dries.

9 When cold, the jars should be labelled and the date shown.

10 Finally, store the jars in a cool dry place.

Jelly-Making

The method for jelly-making is very similar to the above. However, only the juice of the fruit is used; therefore after Step 3 above (i.e. the stewing of the fruit) the fruit should be placed in a jelly-bag and allowed to drain overnight. The bag should not be squeezed as this will force some of the pulp through and make a cloudy jelly. Reheat the juice before adding the warmed sugar and then follow the basic procedure for jam-making, i.e. Step 5 onwards.

Country Wine-making

Using the wild harvest to make wine is a very rewarding pastime and first class results can be achieved if the standard procedures are followed carefully. There is no need to spend more than is necessary on equipment and although the initial outlay may seem high, this is quickly offset by the quality of the end product.

Basic Equipment

A plastic bin or container 'Wine-making' or 'brewing' bins can be purchased quite cheaply and are usually able to hold 2–5 gallons (9–23 litres). A plastic bucket will do, providing that it is white, otherwise dyes in coloured containers may spoil the wine.

Straining cloth It is essential to use a fine sieve for straining and it is best to buy the nylon straining bags made for the wine-maker, some of which are made to fit the standard fermenting bins.

Fermenting jars These are commonly referred to as 'demi-john' jars, and usually have a capacity of 1 gallon (4.5 litres). They are made of either clear or coloured glass: red wines should be placed in coloured jars, if they are to retain their true colour. Fermenting jars can be 'out of action' for months at a time, so quite a few are needed if different wines are to be tried.

Fermentation traps or air-locks One air-lock is needed for each jar and the plastic ones are best for the beginner since the glass type tend to break easily. There are various types available on the market and rubber stoppers can be purchased which not only fit the fermentation jars but have holes already bored in them for the insertion of an air-lock.

Funnel A decent-sized funnel is essential and again the plastic ones are far more durable than those made of glass.

Bottles Although suitable bottles can be bought, it is far cheaper to re-use empty wine bottles. A good supply can be built up from friends and relatives, which should last a long time.

Corks and corking machine Corks of the correct size are readily available and cheap; they are usually sold in packets of a dozen but a bulk purchase of good quality corks would be more economical. A corking machine is not absolutely necessary, but makes corking far easier and reduces the risk of corks coming off when under pressure.

Siphoning tube This takes the form of clear plastic tubing about 6 ft (2 m) in length and of the order of $\frac{3}{8}$ of an inch (1 cm) in diameter. These are available quite cheaply.

Large saucepan In many recipes, a large quantity of boiling water is required; a 1 gallon (4.5 litre) saucepan is ideal, although the rather bigger aluminium 'jam-pans' are better since they hold much more. They are also essential for jam- or jelly-making, of course.

Stirring spoon Although wooden spoons can be used, they tend to stain easily. Plastic ones are better and are easier to clean.

Cleaning chemicals It is very important that all equipment used in wine-making is chemically clean before use. Modern products are able to clean and sterilize in one operation and are recommended. Wine-makers who also have young babies will find the chemicals used for sterilizing babies' bottles equally good.

Yeast and nutrient Nowadays it is possible to buy specially formulated yeast compounds already containing nutrient, which is necessary to obtain the best possible fermentation. A beginner would be well advised to use these initially, before moving on to the more specialized wine yeasts.

Other useful ingredients Campden tablets, wine tannin, citric acid and pectic enzyme are also sometimes used in country wine-making. They do not cost much and last a long time.

General Procedures

Although there are slight variations, making country wines generally involves the following procedures.

Extracting the flavour This may involve crushing, boiling or soaking the main ingredient in hot or cold water. Individual recipes demand different methods, and these should be followed carefully.

Adding sugar and other ingredients The required amount of sugar is dissolved in the liquor and often other ingredients are necessary. The addition of grape concentrate, for example, will improve the vinosity and flavour of the wine. Sometimes there is insufficient acid, which is vital for a good fermentation; citric acid or fruit juice (e.g. lemon juice) is then added to provide this requirement. In a few recipes, pectic enzyme is added; this helps to extract the flavour from the fruit and also ensures a clearer wine. Care must be taken, however, since it must be added when the liquid is cool and 24 hours before the addition of the yeast.

Adding the yeast and nutrient The liquor must be cool (about 21°C, 70°F) before adding the yeast and nutrient, otherwise the yeast may be killed. The addition of a small quantity of grape tannin at this stage improves the taste of most wines.

The initial fermentation The container is closely covered and the liquor allowed to ferment for up to 10 days in a warm place (21°C, 70°F). This fermentation can be quite vigorous.

Straining into fermenting jar The liquor is strained through a fine nylon sieve to the bottom of the neck of the fermenting jar and an air-lock is fitted. It is then allowed to ferment for several weeks, but at a slightly cooler temperature than before (16°C, 60°F).

Racking The wine is racked for the first time when it seems to have cleared. This involves siphoning off the wine from the deposit at the bottom of the jar; it is a very important process if clear wine is to be produced. After racking, the wine should be topped up to the neck again with a syrup made from 3 oz (75 g) of sugar dissolved in ½ pint (300 ml) of water. The air-lock is re-fitted and the racking procedure repeated a few months later.

Bottling A third rack may be necessary before bottling, depending on the amount of sediment at the bottom of the jar. Otherwise, siphon off the wine into clean bottles, remembering to use dark bottles for the red wines. Cork and store the bottles on their sides (ideally on a wine rack) in a cool place (10°C, 50°F or below).

NATURE'S WILD HARVEST

Spring

Alexanders
Smyrnium olusatrum

The habitat of this herbaceous perennial is waste places and the like, particularly in coastal regions where it is often locally abundant. Examples are the sea cliffs at Dover, close by the sea in Norfolk, and the south-west coast of Anglesey. Alexanders, however, can also be found near estuaries, and near to rivers with a high salinity. By February the young, bright glossy green, leaflets are often in evidence; far earlier than those of other wayside plants. By April the plant has reached a height of 3 to 4 feet (1 to 1.3 metres). The stem is solid, round, furrowed, and branched. The large radicle leaves are 3-4 ternate, and the shiny ovate leaflets are cut and coarsely toothed. At the base of the leaf stalk is a broad and very conspicuous membranous sheath with a hairy margin. Flowering continues from late April to June when dense crowded clusters of greenish-yellow flowers are borne in both lateral and terminal umbels. A month later the dark brown or blackish ridged aromatic fruits are to be seen.

The generic name *Smyrnium* is synonymous with myrrh; and the specific name *olusatrum* is derived from *olus*, 'pot-herb', and *atrum*, 'black' (this must surely refer to the colour of the ripened fruit and not to the plant).

It is said that alexanders has an agreeable odour, smelling of celery, but this is a matter for personal opinion. Certainly the plant was cultivated by our forefathers, but it was quickly forgotten with the introduction of more succulent vegetables such as celery.

The young shoots should be picked for eating in winter and early spring. To remove any bitterness, boil in water for 3 minutes, drain and reboil in salted boiling water for a further 7 minutes. Serve with melted butter. They make an excellent spring vegetable, having the flavour of asparagus. The very young leaves can be eaten raw in salads or in sandwiches.

Common Bistort
Polygonum bistorta

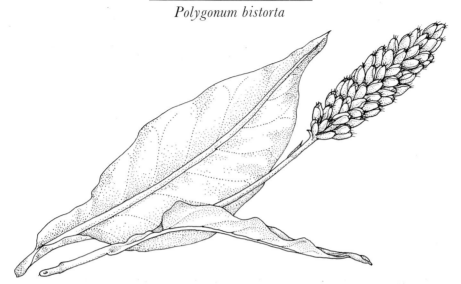

Common bistort is an herbaceous perennial that grows wild in moist meadows or similar situations, but it may also be found as a garden escape. The period of flowering extends from late May through to September, during which time the beds of Bistort display their small terminal cylinders of tiny pink flowers on tall, 1 to 2 feet (30 to 61 cm), stiff stems. Each cylinder is about 1½ to 2 inches (4 to 5 cm) in length and comprises several hundred blossoms. Flowering starts at the base of the cylinder and under a lens it will be seen that the flowers are set in pairs, and are not all alike. The rich pink flowers are perfect and double-sexed; the others are male flowers, smaller, paler and temporarily staying in bud. As the perfect flowers begin to wither and die, so the imperfect ones begin to open successfully. The flower stem is simple with two or three small and stalkless, egg-shaped upper leaves. The larger lower leaves are 6 to 7 inches (15 to 17 cm) long, dark green, pointed and often almost heart-shaped; they have a strong midrib of pale shining green that is very prominent on the back of the leaf. A large and twisted thick black root ramifies underground, so annually enlarging the 'bed area'. The word *bistorta*, meaning 'twice writhen', is derived from the plant's twisted roots.

The leaves, which are rich in vitamin C together with A and B, can be boiled as a vegetable but are traditionally used as the main ingredient in a spring herb pudding by the people of the Lake District. A beer made from the green plant leaves, nettles and dandelion leaves was once drunk by country children as a tonic.

The young shoots are excellent as a pot-herb early in the spring at Eastertime, hence the local names 'Easter Giants' and 'Easter Magiants'. It is also known as 'Snakeweed' and 'Adderwort' because of its twisted roots. Even today it is commonly referred to as 'Patience Dock' or 'Passion Dock'.

In years gone by both the roots and the leaves, in the form of a distillation or powder, were used to treat measles and smallpox, to fasten the teeth in the gums and to stem the bleeding of wounds. Bistort is known to be a strong vegetable astringent.

Bistort pudding

Bistort leaves
Dandelion leaves
Nettle leaves
1 oz (25 g) boiled barley
1 hard-boiled egg
$\frac{1}{2}$ oz (15 g) butter
Pepper and salt

Pick only the young leaves of bistort, dandelion and nettle and cover them with boiling water for 20 minutes. Drain off the water and chop the leaves. Add the boiled barley to the mixture, together with the chopped hard-boiled egg and butter. Season with salt and pepper and stir well. Reheat and place in a pudding basin. This herb pudding is excellent with bacon or veal.

Broom
Cytisus scoparius

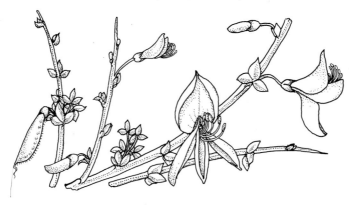

A dry sandy soil with a certain amount of humus, as found on heathland, is what the broom enjoys. This beautiful evergreen shrub grows up to heights of about 6 feet (180 cm), and may also occur on dry rocky hillsides, railway embankments, or even in hedgerows. Its stems are bright or dark green, erect, furrowed, and angular, with many silky branches. The short-stalked, oblong, green leaves may be single or comprised of 3 silky leaflets; they are small and sometimes absent, the stems performing their function to a certain degree. From late April to June the large golden-yellow flowers are produced in thousands, emitting an acacia-like scent. They have the usual butterfly-shape of the pea family (*Leguminosae*), with a large upper petal, two smaller 'wing' petals, and two lower petals which together form a 'keel' to the flower. They produce a black pod bordered with hairs, which contains many seeds; the valves become twisted after opening. The seeds are automatically dispersed from the dry pod for some distance, due to the sudden jerky movement produced when it bursts open.

Cytisus is an old Greek name given to a kind of clover; *scoparius* is from the Latin *scopae*, a 'broom'. The common name of broom alludes to the customary use of making brooms or besoms from the plant's switch branches. The fibrous stem has been manufactured into cloth; and also used quite successfully for thatching.

Broom buds until recent times were regarded as a delicacy and were served as an appetizer at feasts. If gathered in bud in late April or May, they can be pickled or added to salads, whereas on the continent the roasted seeds have been used as a substitute for coffee. Before the introduction of hops, the buds formed an essential ingredient in beer-making, because the sap which runs through the plant's tissues added the necessary bitter tang.

Medicinally the young shoots were often used by country folk as a cure for dropsy. Other common names include Beesom and Breeam; breeam tea, an infusion made from young branch tips, was used as a diuretic (a medicine to stimulate the discharge of urine).

Charlock or Field Mustard
Sinapis arvensis

A sand-loving, shrubby but compact annual that is very common in cultivated land, especially in fields of corn which are often bathed in sulphur yellow during the summer months, so profuse is the growth of this plant. It is not, however, confined solely to arable land and can be found growing quite commonly by the roadside in the company of poppies, on wasteland and on manure stacks. Field mustard may grow to 18 inches (45 cm) tall, the stem is thick, covered in rough hairs, the lower part tinged with purplish-white. Halfway up it very often branches into two parts, and is purplish at the joints. Its lower leaves are petiolate (have a leaf stalk), somewhat lobed, rough and toothed; the upper ones are sessile (stalkless), undivided and finely toothed. From May until August its bright-yellow flower clusters are in evidence almost everywhere. The many-angled seed pods are almost cylindrical, smooth and jointed, and they grow to three times the length of the conical beak. The seeds are black and numerous, and when the pods open they are scattered around the parent plant. Like all mustards the field mustard is very pungent; the flavour of its seeds is hot and acrid, not quite so acceptable as those mustards grown for the table. In Yorkshire it is also called Runsh; other common names are Cherlock and

Garlock. The Latin name *Synapis* alludes to its turnip-like aspect; *arvensis* means 'belonging to arable land'.

During times of hardship and famine in Britain, charlock has been eaten by entire communities, since it is rich in vitamins A, B and C, and provides the necessary bulk and fibre so often missing in present-day diets. To prepare as a vegetable, only the younger leaves should be picked. Simmer them in salted water, strain and serve with a good knob of butter, as an excellent substitute for spinach.

Coltsfoot
Tussilago farfara

This clay-loving herbaceous perennial grows to little more than 6 inches (15 cm) tall even when in flower, and can be found flourishing on railway embankments, the sides of streams, and many other places that offer a steady supply of water during springtime. The stalk is clothed in a spiral of purplish-brown, triangular bracts, and coated with cotton hairs. At the end of February it pushes its way up through the soil, its drooping head carrying a single flower bud, and not a leaf to be seen. The Coltsfoot is very early to flower, first appearing in March and continuing into May. At first sight it might be mistaken for a small dandelion about 1 inch (25 mm) across, but after closer inspection the many differences become apparent. The yellow fringe around the central disc comprises over 300 ray florets arranged in several rows, which have no stamens and are obviously female. On the other hand the central florets (of which there are about 40), forming the yellow disc, have the form of tiny bells. Each has a mouth shaped like a 5-pointed star, the stamen head rising from the centre producing pollen, and although some may have an ovary and column they never form fruit.

At night-time when the flowers close, the fringe tips of the ray florets become dusted with pollen from the central florets; and so, in the early morning as the flowers again open, the pollen mass slides down the ray florets making contact with, and so fertilizing, the ovary column. Insects too bring about fertilization by transferring pollen from adjacent flowers. During heavy falls of rain the coltsfoot droops its head letting the sheath of bracts bear the brunt of the weather, and so protecting the pollen. As the flowers fade and die so their heads close and hang a little, the ovaries during this time become brown and hard, and it is now that the stalk becomes erect once more, and a feather-brush of white hairs appears; not so beautiful as the dandelion's 'clock' but equally effective in dispersing the seed that is suspended from the end of each hair. It is not until now that the leaves begin to appear from underground, first as soft downy-white spear-like protrusions which subsequently develop into large, broad, round to heart-shaped leaves; they are toothed and coated in a thick white down on both surfaces, the down later rubbing off from the upper surface to reveal a green and comparatively smooth leaf. It has numerous underground shoots, which are long and ending in suckers; the plant spreads extensively by virtue of its burrowing stolons.

The generic name *Tussilago* is from the Latin *tussis* 'a cough', relating to its acclaim as a cough cure; *farfara* is a Latin name for the plant. Its common name of coltsfoot alludes to the shape of the leaf; other names attributed to it include Clayweed, Coughwort, and Cleats which is the name of a beer made from it. The plant has long been used as a cough remedy, with coltsfoot lozenges a firm favourite a century ago. Its leaves smoked through a reed were once used to remove mucus in the chest and to relieve catarrh. The dried roots were burnt to repel gnats and other troublesome flying insects.

The flowers are richly honey-scented and of great medicinal value. Gather them on a dry day. They make an excellent wine, used fresh or dried; dry at a temperature of 38°C (100°F).

Coltsfoot flower wine

7 pints (4 l) flower heads
3 lb (1.5 kg) sugar
7 pints (4 l) water
2 oranges
1 lemon
Grape tannin (1 teaspoon)
Yeast and nutrient

Warm the water in a large pan and stir in the sugar until completely dissolved. Bring the solution to the boil and simmer for 5 minutes. Allow to cool to room temperature before stirring in the thinly peeled rind of oranges and lemon, the juice from these, the grape tannin and the flower heads. Mix the yeast and nutrient in a little of the liquid and stir into the mixture. Cover closely and leave in a warm place for a week, stirring daily. Strain through a nylon sieve into a fermenting jar and fit an air-lock. Bottle when the wine has cleared.

Cow Parsley or Wild Chervil
Anthriscus sylvestris

This herbaceous perennial can be found growing in rich soil along hedgebanks, the borders of fields, wooded areas and shaded places in general. The stem is branched and stout, reaching heights of between 2 and 4 feet (60 and 120 cm), it is hairy below and smooth above, hollow, furrowed, and carries many leaves; it is swollen below the nodes. The leaves are bi- or tri-pinnate, and the leaflets are divided almost to the base. It has green, lanceolate bracteoles (tiny leaves growing out beneath the calyx from the flower stems), which are fringed with hairs, spreading or turned back. The flowers are small and white, growing in stalked umbels terminally. They can appear as early as March but more usually from April to June. The flower clusters are drooping at first but soon become erect. The oblong petals are inversely egg-shaped and hooded. Its oblong fruits with their very short beaks begin to appear from June onwards, the foliage by now having become a dark and rather dull green.

The entire plant is somewhat aromatic, and a favourite food of the rabbit. The leaves are readily eaten and enjoyed by cattle, and quite wholesome to humans; yet the roots are said to be poisonous, with a few reports of death when eaten as parsnip. Both leaves and flowers produce a dye. It is also known as Wild Beaked Parsley.

Do not confuse cow parsley with hemlock (*Conium maculatum*), which is a poisonous sand-loving biennial that grows by streams, rivers, roadsides and on waste places. It can grow up to 8 ft (2.5 m), twice the height of cow parsley. The smooth hollow stem is finely furrowed, is bluish white with purple spots and has many branches. The leaves are triangular and divided into many lanceolate leaflets with sharp coarse teeth. The umbels of several hundred tiny white flowers are only in bloom during June and July. If eaten, hemlock can cause dizziness, vomiting or headaches.

Pick the young cow parsley shoots and use fresh in spring salads or boiled as a vegetable. They can be dried and used throughout the year in a vegetable soup.

Dandelion
Taraxacum officinale

This widespread perennial grows to a height of around 8 inches (20 cm) and is perhaps typically found in moist meadowland, although one form prefers wet marshy areas, and yet another shows a preference for drier soils; it is often seen growing along the feet of walls, and in waste places almost everywhere. Its hollow flower-stalks are round, smooth, succulent, juicy and leafless, bearing just one flower. The bright green leaves emanate from the root forming a rosette; they are deeply divided with backward-pointing lobes, and ruggedly toothed, except towards the leaf base, where the margin is just jagged. Flowers appear from March or April to October, the flowerheads are broad, 1 to 2 inches (2.5 to 5 cm) across, bright golden-yellow, and composed of between 100 and 300 florets; they close at night-time or when rain threatens. Light intensity seems to determine at what hour they open during early morning. The involucre (whorl of bracts that encloses the bud) is bell-shaped, the

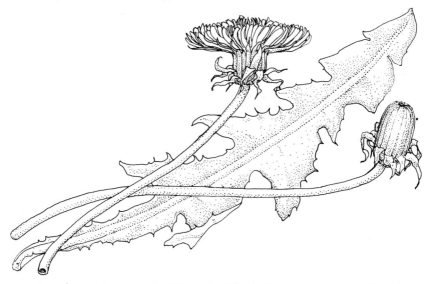

outer scales turning downwards. When the flower dies, its orange petals wither and are pushed away in a bunch by the rapidly growing base of the calyx, and now the old flowerheads look almost as they did when in bud. A sudden transformation is about to take place, when, from within the involucre, a truly beautiful gossamer ball will appear. This is composed of many dozen silver hairs each attached at the base to a seed and is ready, at the first gust of wind, to break up and fly away. The silvery ball of gossamer threads is commonly called a 'clock'.

The common name comes from the French *dent de lion*, a fanciful suggestion that its leaf is like the tooth of a lion, but it may more probably allude to the likeness of the sun's rays to the plant's golden-yellow flower, the lion being symbolic of the sun. The generic name *Taraxacum* could be derived from the Greek *tarasso*, 'I disturb', referring to the dandelion's medicinal effects; the specific name *officinale* is also from the Latin and alludes to its use in medicine.

Our forefathers had a very high opinion of the dandelion; for them it was food and medicine. The leaves are rich in vitamins A and C and they also contain vitamin B_1. They are slightly acrid but if the leaves are blanched (covered to exclude daylight) during growth they become whitish in colour. Then they make an excellent addition to salads and can also be eaten in sandwiches. In spring, the tender young leaves make an acceptable vegetable when boiled. The flowerheads are used in wine-making and the whole plant is used in the famous dandelion beer. A coffee made from the roots is said to be almost indistinguishable from real coffee, and even an improvement on some of the inferior blends; it is also free from caffeine. To prepare it, dry the young roots, clean and roast them in a moderate oven. Allow to cool and then grind. Pour boiling water over the grounds, stir and leave for 10 minutes before straining.

Herbalists use the plant extensively because it has mild diuretic and laxative properties and is excellent in treating anaemia and poor blood conditions. A tonic made from the roots and leaves is useful for liver troubles and fevers, as well as being good for the complexion. The diuretic properties of the dandelion are captured by the English name 'Wet-a-bed' which reveals the effect of the plant on the kidneys and the bladder.

Dandelion wine

5 pints (3 l) flower heads
3 lb (1.5 kg) sugar
7 pints (4 l) water
4 oranges
Yeast and nutrient

Soak the flower heads in the boiling water and leave for no more than 2 days. Add the orange peel and bring the mixture to the boil, simmering for 10–15 minutes. Strain through a nylon sieve onto the sugar, stirring continuously to dissolve it completely. Allow to cool to room temperature, before adding the orange juice, yeast and nutrient. Pour into a fermenting jar and fit an air-lock. Bottle when the wine has cleared.

Dandelion beer

1 lb (500 g) dandelion plants
2 lb (1 kg) sugar
7 pints (4 l) water
2 lemons
$\frac{1}{2}$ oz (15 g) root ginger
1 oz (25 g) cream of tartar
2 teaspoons granulated yeast

This is best prepared during the spring, and the entire plant may be used. Place the dandelion, root ginger and finely peeled rind of both lemons in a pan with all the water and boil for 15 minutes. Strain onto the sugar and cream of tartar, stirring well to dissolve all the sugar. Leave covered to cool to room temperature before adding the lemon juice and granulated yeast. Cover again and leave for a further 3–4 days in a warm place. Bottle using screw-capped bottles. It is essential to store these in a cool place at this stage, for no more than a week. If kept at too high a temperature the bottles may burst; if left for too long, the beer may become flat.

Dandelion syrup

8 oz (250 g) dandelion flowers
8 oz (250 g) sugar
¾ pint (450 ml) water

Boil the water and pour over the flower heads. Cover and leave for 24 hours. Strain the mixture and stir in the sugar until dissolved. Simmer gently until the mixture reaches a syrup consistency. Pour into sterilized bottles when cold.

Garlic Mustard or Sauce Alone
Alliaria petiolata

A familiar annual plant of the roadside hedges which thrives on a sandy soil with a fair humus content. It ranges in height from 2 to 3 feet (60 to 90 cm) with an erect stem. The first leaves to appear are rounded and very like those of the violet, but much larger and of a paler green; the stem leaves are large, broadly heart-shaped, strongly veined, deeply toothed at the margin, giving the leaf a notched appearance, and on long foot-stalks. From May to June the flattened clusters of small white flowers are much in evidence, their four petals resembling a cross (hence the family name *Cruciferae*, which includes the 'cresses' and the 'brassicas' etc). The fruit of the garlic mustard takes the form of stiff, slightly curved, narrow pods that stand out like horns of an inch (2.5 cm) or more in length, and contain a number of seeds. If the leaves are bitten into, their hot juices burn the tongue as would mustard; if they are crushed or bruised, a strong smell of garlic becomes very apparent—hence the name garlic mustard. Other common names regularly in use include 'Jack-by-the-hedge', 'Hedge Garlic' and 'Flixweed'. Our forefathers used it as a vegetable to boil with meat, hence the name 'Sauce Alone'.

The garlic taste is mild and ideal for flavouring. The leaves, chopped finely, give added zest to salads and make an excellent sandwich filling. A spring sauce, made by chopping the leaves with a little mint and hawthorn buds and mixing with vinegar and sugar, is good especially when served with lamb. In Wales, the leaves are eaten with fried bacon or herrings. The young leaves and shoots should be picked in March and April, washed thoroughly and boiled until tender (approximately 3-5 minutes). Drain and serve tossed in melted butter.

The seeds have been used to promote sneezing (probably when ground into a powder). It was used as a sudorific (a medicine that causes a person to sweat) and as an antiseptic. The leaves, applied externally, were supposed to cure soreness of the throat. It is a very undesirable plant when growing in pastureland, for if cows feed upon it their milk becomes flavoured with garlic; if poultry eat it their flesh also becomes unpleasing to the palate.

Gorse or Furze
Ulex europaeus

Gorse is an evergreen perennial shrub with green branches, usually reaching a height of about 6 feet (180 cm), but in sheltered positions occasionally growing to 15 or even 18 feet (4.5 to 5.5 metres). It is particularly suited by the dry sandy conditions of heathland, especially in a humus soil. Gorse is a very dense, and much branched, stunted shrub; which in its later stages is void of leaves, these having changed into very long, slender, sharp spines. The green stem is spreading and hairy;

Dulse
Rhodymenia palmata

Sea Kale
Crambe maritima

Bistort
Polygonum bistorta

Sea Beet
Beta vulgaris maritima

Carragheen Moss
Chondrus crispus

Coltsfoot
Tussilago farfara

Dandelion
Taraxacum officinale

Charlock
Sinapis arvensis

Broom
Cytisus scoparius

Stinging Nettle
Urtica dioica

Cow Parsley
Anthriscus sylvestris

Garlic Mustard
Alliaria petiolata

Sweet Cicely
Myrrhis odorata

Gorse
Ulex europaeus

Alexanders
Smyrnium olusatrum

Morel
Morchella esculenta

St. George's Mushroom
Tricholoma gambosum

Hawthorn Blossom
Crataegus monogyna

the hairs protect the water pores, which lie hidden in long furrows, from becoming waterlogged during periods of heavy rain. Water pores in most plants are mainly found on the foliage. Only in very young gorse plants do we find ordinary soft green leaves, which are composed of three leaflets; but after a short time the leaves produced are much narrower and stiffer, and eventually nothing more than green spines. The calyx is yellow and shaggy with black hairs.

The golden yellow flowers are extremely numerous, and are borne upon the spines; they appear from April to August, but in some years can be seen in just about every month. Outside they are clothed in two large yellow sepals; the five petals are of the usual butterfly-shape peculiar to the pea family, with a large upper petal, the wings and keel petals interlocking; the wing petals being larger than those of the keel. Its black pods are clothed with brownish hairs, and they burst open when mature, the explosion scattering the seeds some distance. The seeds are further dispersed by ants. There seems to be no apparent reason why *Ulex* should have been given as the generic name; the specific name, however, refers to the plant's European distribution. Other common names are Whin, Prickly Broom, Gorst or Goss; and in Devon Vuzz.

Gorse was once deliberately cultivated as fodder for horses, cows and sheep. Bakers used it as a fuel for their ovens and in Ireland the flowers were used to flavour whisky. A sweet tea can be made by infusing two tablespoons of freshly-picked flowers in $\frac{3}{4}$ pint (450 ml) of boiling water, straining before drinking. The flowers also make an excellent wine.

Gorse wine

1 gallon (4.5 l) flowers
3 lb (1.5 kg) sugar
2 lemons
1 orange
7 pints (4 l) water
1 teaspoon grape tannin
Yeast and nutrient

Bring the water to the boil and pour over the flowers. Simmer for 15 minutes before straining, extracting as much liquid as possible. Add the sugar, the finely peeled rind of the fruit and their juice, stirring well to dissolve all the sugar. Allow to cool to room temperature before adding the wine tannin, yeast and nutrient. Cover closely and keep in a warm place for 2–3 days, stirring daily. Strain into a fermenting jar and fit an air-lock. Keep in a cool place and rack after about 3 months. This wine may require racking several times if it is to clear well.

Stinging Nettle
Urtica dioica

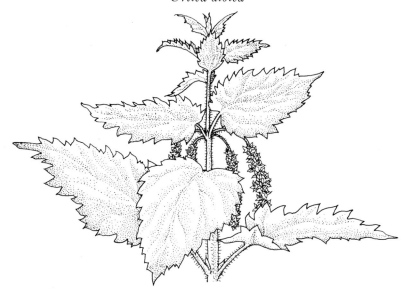

Although essentially a sand-loving plant, the nettle also thrives on almost any waste land close to dwelling places, quickly inhabiting rubbish heaps and other untended areas. It may be encountered along our roadsides, or growing in clumps in fields and meadows, particularly where high manuring has occurred. The plant ranges in height from 2 to 4 feet (61 to 122 cm), is unisexual and perennial. Its leaves are ovate, pointed, and deeply toothed along the margin. They are strongly veined and set in opposite pairs horizontally to the stalk with each leaf pair at right angles to its neighbouring pair, the lower leaves having slightly longer stems than the upper ones. Each leaf is covered with forward-pointing, stinging hairs; each hair is but a long tube set on a cushion of delicate tissue, and contains a virulent juice composed mainly of formic acid and an enzyme. When you are stung by a nettle the acid causes the burning sensation and the enzyme produces the white blister. Flowering occurs from July to September; the females are greenish in dense catkin-like clusters and the male plants produce loose panicles of slightly yellower flowers than the females. In both sexes the flowers hang in rings from the leaf nodes.

Nettle fibres were much used a century or more ago, especially so in northern Britain when nettle sheets and nettle table cloths were fashioned, and nettle fibres were used as thread. The name nettle is derived from the Anglo-Saxon words *netel* or *naedl* meaning something with which one sews. In olden days whipping with nettles was practised as a relief for rheumatic pains and the like.

Nettles have important nutritional value as they are rich in vitamins A and C. The formic acid which gives rise to the nettle sting is destroyed during cooking, so that the nettle can be eaten as a vegetable in the same way as spinach. Only the tops should be used and these must be picked before the plant starts flowering in June. They should be washed well and then boiled in very little water until tender. Drain off the water, chop, add a little butter and seasoning and they make an excellent green vegetable.

Its medicinal importance has long been recognized and during the Second World War over 90 tons were gathered for County Herb Committees. Nettle tea is a tonic rich in vitamins and essential minerals. To make the tea, add 2 teaspoons of dried nettle flowers to $\frac{3}{4}$ pint (450 ml) of boiling water and infuse for 3 minutes before straining. If allowed to cool, it can also be used as a soothing lotion for nettle rash, burns and sunburn.

Nettle pudding

7 pints (4 l) young nettle tops
2 large onions
1 small cabbage
4 oz (100 g) rice

Wash the nettle tops thoroughly and mix with the chopped onion and cabbage. Place the mixture in alternate layers with the rice in a muslin bag, and secure tightly. Lower this into a pan of boiling salted water and boil until the vegetables are tender. The pudding is best served with gravy or butter.

Nettle soup

$\frac{1}{2}$ pint (300 ml) young nettle tops
1 onion
1 large potato
1 oz (25 g) butter or margarine
1 pint (600 ml) stock
$\frac{1}{2}$ pint (300 ml) milk
Salt and pepper

Dice the potato, chop the onion and gently fry both in the butter. Chop the nettles finely and add them with the stock to the mixture. Season with salt and pepper and simmer for 20 minutes. Add the milk, re-heat and use further seasoning if necessary.

Creamed nettles

½ pint (300 ml) young nettle tops
2 oz (50 g) butter or margarine
2 teaspoons chopped chives or spring onions
1 tablespoon cream or top of the milk
Salt and pepper

Wash and dry the nettle tops and discard the stalks. Put the leaves and the chives into a pan with the butter and simmer gently on a low heat, stirring occasionally until the nettles are all well-buttered and tender. Sprinkle with salt and pepper. Drain off the juices, add a knob of butter and the cream or top of the milk. Re-heat before serving.

Nettle wine

4 pints (2.5 l) young nettle tops
3½ lb (1.5 kg) sugar
7 pints (4 l) water
2 lemons
½ oz (15 g) root ginger
Yeast and nutrient

Wash the young nettle tops and simmer in 2 pints (1.2 l) of water with the ginger and thinly peeled rind of both lemons. After about three-quarters of an hour, strain and add the remaining water to the juice. Stir in the sugar and lemon juice, making sure that the sugar is completely dissolved. Allow to cool to room temperature before adding the yeast and nutrient. Cover closely and leave for 3-4 days in a warm place, stirring daily. Pour into a fermenting jar and fit an air-lock. Rack for the first time when the wine begins to clear and leave for a further few months before bottling.

Nettle syrup

1 lb (500 g) young nettle tops
2 pints (1.2 l) water
Sugar

Wash the nettles well and place in a pan with the water. Boil for an hour and then strain. Measure the liquid and add 1 lb (500 g) of sugar to every pint (600 ml) of juice. Boil for a further 30 minutes and allow to cool before bottling.

Sweet Cicely
Myrrhis odorata

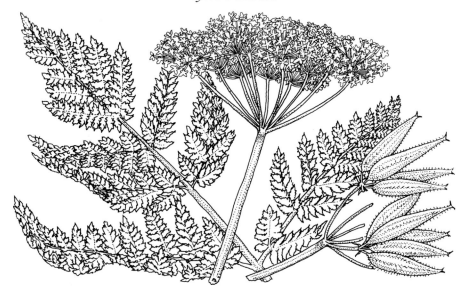

Perhaps more commonly met with in northern England and the Scottish Lowlands, this herbaceous perennial is to be found growing in dry hilly pastures, along waysides and hedgerows. Its habit is erect, growing from 2 to 3 feet (60 to 90 cm) tall; the stout stem is hollow and grooved. The large triangular leaves are three-times pinnate, its lance-shaped leaflets are pinnatified (feather-cleft, i.e. divided almost to the base); they are somewhat downy below, blotched but bright and glossy above, and when crushed smell of aniseed. It flowers from May to June, the large terminal flower-heads bearing numerous white florets whose petals are bent slightly inwards; the bracts are lance-shaped. The large fruits are beaked, roughly ridged, about 1 inch (2.5 cm) long, dark brown, and very fragrant. It has also been known as Sweet Chervil.

The entire plant can be eaten when boiled as a vegetable and the leaves which taste of anise can be used in salads. The leaves can be dried and added to soups and stews, and to vegetables such as cabbage and spinach to improve their taste. The seeds are the most aromatic part of the plant and may be chewed or used as a flavouring; they are a mild laxative. In the past, the seeds have been used to polish oak floors and furniture, particularly in the North of England.

The leaves of sweet cicely are an excellent substitute for sugar and are ideal for sweetening acid fruits such as rhubarb and gooseberries, as they replace half the amount of sugar normally added, as well as imparting additional flavour to the fruit. It is also used in the making of various liqueurs, including Chartreuse. The root of the plant may be eaten and was once thought to be a safeguard against the plague.

A useful tonic which aids digestion and stimulates the appetite can be made by simmering the leaves in a saucepan with water for 3 minutes. The tonic should be left overnight and then drunk unstrained, a wineglassful at a time. The tea is useful for coughs, flatulence and stomach complaints.

Sweet Cicely wine

2 pints (1.2 l) sweet cicely leaves
1 pint (600 ml) grapefruit juice (unsweetened)
$2\frac{1}{2}$ lb (1.25 kg) sugar
7 pints (4 l) water
$\frac{1}{4}$ teaspoon wine tannin
Yeast and nutrient

Heat the water and stir in the sugar until dissolved; bring to the boil and pour onto the sweet cicely leaves. Cover and allow to cool to room temperature. Stir in the fruit juice, tannin, yeast and nutrient. Cover again, and leave in a warm place for a week. Strain into a fermenting jar and fit an air-lock. Rack for the first time when the wine clears and bottle after about 6 months.

Common Hawthorn
Crataegus monogyna

Hawthorn is common throughout the British Isles, and *Crataegus monogyna* is the most widespread of all the European hawthorns. Few people can be unfamiliar with its late May or June blossom, often profuse, and with that peculiar scent that has been likened to the smell of 'herrings', produced by trimethylamine which is present in the flowers. The fruit, when ripe, is in the form of small red berries or 'haws', which if squeezed between finger and thumb reveal a single stone. As a windbreak the hawthorn hedge proves very satisfactory and it still provides the cheapest and best hedge, so well suited as a field boundary.

The Midland Hawthorn (*Crataegus oxyacanthoides*) is so named because only in our Midland counties is it really common. It is most often met with in moist woodlands and much less used for hedges.

The young leaves have a pleasant nutty taste and chopped up with the flower buds they impart added flavour to beetroot and potato salads. Herbalists use the berries and leaves to produce a tonic for the heart.

Hawthorn blossom liqueur

Hawthorn blossom
Brandy or whisky
1 tablespoon sugar
Water

Pick the blossom on a dry sunny day and press down into a 1 lb (500 g) Kilner jar until full. Cover with brandy or whisky and place a cover over the jar; leave for 2 weeks before straining. Dissolve the sugar in as little hot water as possible and mix thoroughly with the whisky or brandy. Pour into sterilized bottles when cold.

Hawthorn blossom wine

4 pints (2.5 l) hawthorn blossom
3 lb (1.5 kg) sugar
2 lemons
7 pints (4 l) water
Grape tannin
Yeast and nutrient

Grate the thinly peeled rind of both lemons and extract the juice from one of them. Add both rind and juice to the sugar and water and boil the mixture for 30 minutes, stirring occasionally. Allow to cool to room temperature before adding the tannin, yeast and nutrient. Leave for a day before adding the flowers; cover and leave for a further week in a warm place, stirring daily. Strain through a fine nylon sieve into a fermenting jar and fit an air-lock. Rack when the wine clears and it should be ready for bottling 3-4 months later.

Common Morel
Morchella esculenta

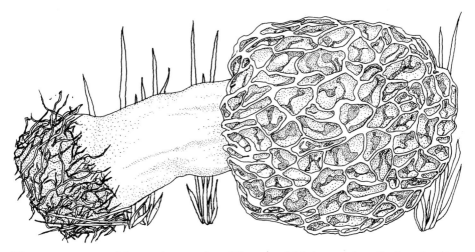

The common morel is a spring species of fungus which is occasionally found under hedgerows, in gardens, on banks and on burnt ground such as bonfire sites. The cap is brownish-grey or ochraceous brown, sub-globose, and hollow, 1 to 1½ inches (3 to 4 cm) wide and 1¼ to 2½ inches (3.5 to 6 cm) long; it is very variable both in shape and colour. The outer surface is honeycombed, consisting of sinuous ridges surrounding shallow, angular and irregularly shaped pits. The stem is 1½ to 3 inches (4 to 8 cm) high, stout, hollow, cylindrical and often thicker at the base; it is minutely scurfy above, longitudinally furrowed, and sullied white. Flesh waxy and brittle with a pleasant taste.

Morels should be thoroughly washed before eating as grit particles tend to stick to the fungus. To prepare for cooking wash in several changes of cold water, boil for a couple of minutes in slightly salted water, then rinse in cold water and wipe dry. When prepared in this way they can either be used fresh or dried for later use; they are then excellent for flavouring stews, soups, sauces and gravies during the rest of the year. They can also be eaten on their own if cooked slowly until tender, but large quantities should not be consumed at any one meal as they can cause indigestion. When picking morels, discard any that are soft, faded or have an unpleasant smell.

Morel sauce

$\frac{3}{4}$ lb (350 g) morels
$\frac{1}{4}$ pint (150 ml) vegetable stock
$\frac{1}{4}$ oz (10 g) flour
1 tablespoon chopped parsley
$\frac{1}{2}$ oz (15 g) butter
Salt and pepper

Slice the morels thinly and place in a pan with the stock; bring to the boil. Melt the butter in a frying pan, add the flour, parsley, salt and pepper, and gently fry for 2 minutes. Then stir this into the morel stock. Simmer gently until the fungi are tender. Serve hot.

St. George's Mushroom
Tricholoma gambosum

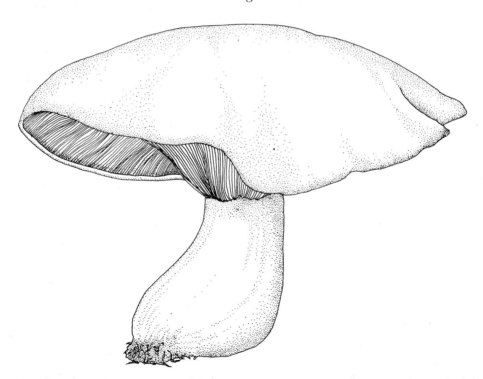

Open grassland and the grassy margins of, and the clearings in, woodland seem to be the principal habitat of St. George's mushroom, especially so on a chalk or limestone soil. This locally common species occurs in groups or rings from April until

June, only rarely met with later in the year. The creamy-white, light buff, or pinkish-buff cap may be 2 to 6 inches (5 to 15 cm) across; it is convex to expanded, smooth with a kid-glove texture, and sometimes deeply split; the margin which is wavy and often inrolled is woolly at first. The cream-coloured gills are crowded and narrow, sinuate or adnate with a decurrent tooth. The flesh and spores are white. The stem is whitish, short, stout, and solid, becoming ochraceous, slightly swollen, and occasionally curved at base. It stands about 3 inches (7.5 cm) tall. When cut, it has the smell of new meal. It derives its common name from St. George's Day, April 23rd, because it can sometimes be seen about that date; but it is more commonly found during the month of May.

St. George's mushrooms are excellent for eating. For use in salads, boil for a couple of minutes only and serve cooled. They can be added to stews, soups and sauces, but when fried in butter, then mixed with an egg yolk and cream, they make a delicious snack on toast. They can be used in all the same ways as mushrooms but require cooking just a little longer to make them tender.

Dried fungi

Any species of edible fungi except saffron milk-caps

Remove the stalks from the larger mushrooms; peel the caps and stalks and cut into thick slices. Small mushrooms can be left whole. Place the fungi in a cool oven to dry. Once dried, crush them in a bowl and then rub through a sieve, to obtain a powder. Store in airtight jars in a cool, dry place. The powder can be used to flavour soups, sauces, stews and casseroles.

Sea Beet or Wild Spinach
Beta vulgaris ssp. *maritima*

This herbaceous perennial is a common seaside plant in England, and it also occurs in Wales and some of Scotland's southern districts. Sea-cliffs, beaches, muddy shores, and salt marshes are its habitat. The lower part of the sea beet's stem is often prostrate before ascending to a tall and succulent growth of up to 3 feet (90 cm); it is numerously branched and angular giving the plant a pyramidal outline. The fleshy, shining, deep green leaves are triangular to egg-shaped before narrowing into a leaf-stalk. From June to October it produces long clustered spikes of small green, sessile, and not very attractive, flowers. These seem mostly to grow singly or in twos, with a small pale green leaf below each flower or pair, and sepals that are bent inwards. The thick fleshy root has a sweet flavour. During autumn many of the leaves take on shades of purple and crimson but some retain their rich green hue. It is considered by many to be a wild form of the cultivated beet.

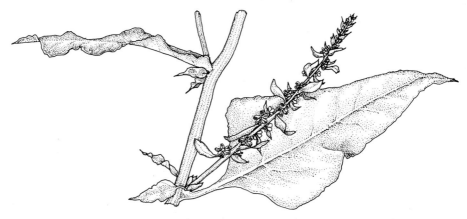

The leaves of sea beet are an excellent vegetable since they are rich in vitamins A and C; they have a long season from April to October, and when cooked and seasoned are tastier than garden spinach. Remember to wash the leaves thoroughly before eating to remove the sand particles which adhere to them. Pick the thin, smaller leaves for eating raw in salads, and the larger leaves for boiling as a vegetable. Chop the leaves, cook them quickly in very little water until tender and serve with a knob of butter.

Sea Kale or Sea Cabbage
Crambe maritima

Found on sandy and shingly sea coasts, particularly in the West of England but by no means confined to that coast. A compact, salt-loving perennial plant very suited for sandy soils, and often growing in the company of Sea Rocket, Sea Purslane, Sea Milkwort and Sea Holly. The root is thick and fleshy; the stem stout with many branches; its bluish-green, rounded leaves are wide, wavy, and toothed. Both stem and leaves are smooth. It grows up to 2 feet (60 cm) tall. The large white flowers are $\frac{1}{2}$ inch (12 mm) across, they grow in corymbs (the stalks of the lower flowers being longer than those of the upper flowers, so that all the flowers of each cluster grow to about the same level), and are in bloom during June, July, and August. The seed pods are ovoid, large, and on slender suberect stalks; they do not open to let the single seeds fall out, but drop to the ground, and so the seeds germinate close to the parent plant. The name *Crambe* is Greek for kale, and *maritima*, which is Latin, refers to the plant's sea coast habitat.

It has been eaten as a vegetable for centuries and indeed during the late eighteenth century it became so popular that large quantities were picked and sent to Covent Garden market for sale. As a result of this intensive collecting it rapidly became depleted and has never recovered its widespread distribution. Thus, it is important that the plant should only be picked where it is common and then not more than three stems from each plant should be taken.

The young shoots begin to push up through the sand in March and can be picked together with the flowering tops from April to June. Discard the leaves, wash the stems and tops well, and boil in salted water until tender. Drain and serve tossed in seasoned butter or in a cheese sauce. The young flowering tops often resemble broccoli when in bud and the taste is similar too. As well as being eaten as a vegetable, the stems, when stripped of the tough leaves, can also be chopped and eaten raw in salads.

Carragheen Moss
Chondrus crispus

Of all the red seaweeds this is the most variable. It grows from a flat disc-like hold-fast and under sheltered conditions is almost without a stalk. The flat, membranous frond is wide and very tough, and its many branches are usually (but not always) divided into two small rounded sections at the extremities; but much depends on the type of habitat. In exposed situations it may be quite narrow, almost rounded in section and have but few branches. Sometimes its growth is so prolific as to form a carpet up to 6 inches (15 cm) thick on the flat rocks of the lower shore zone. When in rock pools it may be quite thin with the frond ends glowing an iridescent violet until removed from the water. In the middle to lower shore it occurs on all but mud. The typical colour is dark red, frequently a dull purple, sometimes pinkish, and during periods of prolonged sunshine it may even be green, except at the base. Even with so many possible variations the overall pattern and frond texture are sufficiently characteristic as to make identification possible after a few careful observations. During the winter months the small swellings of its fruit bodies become apparent. May be readily distinguished from *Gigartina stellata*, another red weed, but whose frond margins are inrolled to form a channel, and which has greater terminal branching. *Chondrus crispus* is adundant and has a wide distribution throughout Europe and the Atlantic coast of North America.

Carragheen Moss
Gigartina stellata

Another common red weed whose growth is often mingled with that of *Chondrus crispus* but from which it may be differentiated by close inspection of the frond margins which are inrolled. It can also be found growing alone, and on the middle and lower shores is quite often the commonest seaweed, frequently covering boulders with its bushy tuft-like growth; particularly on the shores of western Scotland. The very dark brownish-red fronds grow from a circular holdfast and they are from 4 to 8 inches (10 to 20 cm) tall, stem and branches are flat and membranous, the branches repeatedly and equally forked terminally. The fronds may be characteristically dotted with small leaf-like excrescences; these are the fruit bodies emerging from its surface. It is often covered with the grey-brown spiny masses of the polyzoan *Flustrella hispida*, particularly at the base of the fronds; or encrusted with white patches of the Sea Lace, *Membranipora membranacea*. It is a common seaweed, widely distributed in Europe and along the Atlantic coast of North America. Both *Chondrus crispus* and *Gigartina stellata* are sources of agar-agar, a gelatinous non-nitrogenous substance made from seaweed.

Carragheen is best gathered in the spring and it is a source of vegetable gelatine which can be used in both sweet and savoury dishes. It should be washed and then gently boiled in either milk and sugar for sweet recipes, or in water with seasoning for savoury recipes: continue boiling until the seaweed dissolves into a thick jelly. Strain off the liquid and leave it to set. Table jelly, blancmange, ice cream, salad dressing and soups can all be made from carragheen.

When freshly gathered, it can be dried and stored for use at any time. First wash it well and then lay it out in a sheltered position outside so that it can dry. Rinse with fresh water now and again until it finally bleaches to a creamy-white colour. Then it should be brought indoors, dried thoroughly and stored in bags for future use. During the Second World War, the people of Jersey recognized the importance of the seaweed as a valuable supplement to the diet and men were employed to collect and prepare it in large quantities.

Medicinally it is useful in chest and bronchial infections, as well as in the treat-

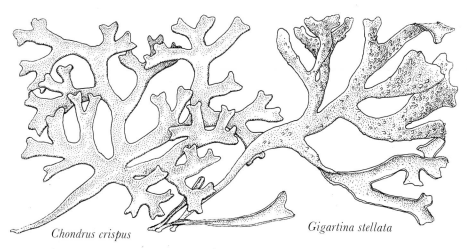

Chondrus crispus   *Gigartina stellata*

ment of stomach ulcers and diseases of the bladder and kidneys. A syrup to combat coughs and colds can be made by adding ¼ cup of rinsed carragheen moss and the thinly pared rind and juice of 2 lemons to 6 cups of water. Boil the mixture for 10 minutes, add a dessertspoonful of honey and simmer for a further 10 minutes before straining. Serve the syrup hot or cold.

Carragheen custard

1 cup soaked carragheen
2½ cups milk
1 egg
1 tablespoon sugar

Soak the carragheen in water for 15 minutes, and after draining off the water add 1–2 cupfuls of milk. Simmer for 30 minutes and strain. Separate the yolk from the white of the egg. Beat the yolk in the remaining cold milk and then mix well into the hot strained carragheen milk. Add the sugar. Beat the egg-white until stiff, then fold into the mixture.

Carragheen jelly

1 cup soaked carragheen
1 pint (600 ml) water
6 oz (150 g) sugar
1 orange
2 lemons
Green colouring

Place the soaked carragheen in a pan with the thinly cut rind of the orange and lemons and boil in the water for 15 minutes. Mix the orange and lemon juice with the sugar and strain the boiling liquid onto it. Add a little green colouring, pour into a mould and allow to set.

Carragheen blancmange

½ cup of dried carragheen moss
1 pint (600 ml) milk
3 teaspoons sugar
1 teaspoon grated lemon rind

Soak the carragheen in water for 15 minutes, then drain it. Place the moss in a pan with the milk and lemon rind and simmer for 30 minutes. Stir in the sugar, pour into a basin or mould, and leave to set.

Dulse
Rhodymenia palmata

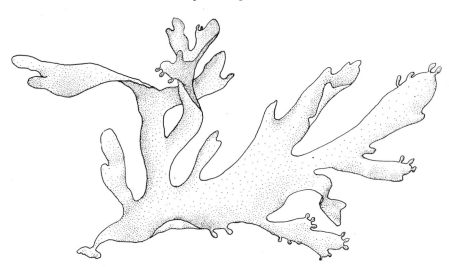

This dull dark red to reddish-brown seaweed shows considerable diversity in shape and size. It may be palmate or just a single blade of varying widths, sometimes with smaller pieces of frond growing from the margin of the main blade. The frond is tough, flat, thin, almost opaque, and emanates without stalk from a disc holdfast; it grows to lengths of 4 to 12 inches (10 to 30 cm). It is found on middle to lower shores where it occurs in thickish tufts on rocks, or smaller pieces may fringe the edge of a pool; when seen under water it exhibits a purplish sheen. It is often found growing in quantity on the stalks of larger weeds such as *Fucus* and *Laminaria*. It is a widely distributed species and very common, occurring in British Isles, Iceland, the northern Mediterranean shores and the Atlantic coast of the USA. This is the edible dulse which the Vikings and early Celtic monks gathered as a source of food.

Another weed, the pepper-dulse, *Laurencia pinnatifida*, is worth mentioning since it is sometimes used in Scotland as a condiment, for its sharp hot taste. The tough leathery fronds are typically purplish-red, with a main stem which is alternately branched; each small branch is similarly divided into very small branchlets. It is very variable, and may be composed of slender branches or small leaf-like ones; in either case their arrangement is similar. It is found very low on the shore, and is usually 3 to 4 inches (7.5 to 10 cm) tall. It also grows on steep middle shore rocks with a sunny aspect, when its colour is usually some shade of yellowish or whitish green, and the growth dense and turf-like.

Another red weed which should be mentioned because of its superficial resemblance to *Rhodymenia palmata* is *Rhodymenia pseudopalmata (palmetta)*. It too is found on the middle and lower shores and although of wide distribution is not a common plant. At 2 to 4 inches (2.5 to 5 cm) tall it is substantially smaller than the edible dulse. It is not so dark red in colour, and has fronds of a similar tough texture, but these are stalked and never have subsidiary growth from margin of main edge. The fronds' branches are about equally divided into two wedge-shaped sections, and these further divided into two rounded tips. It is found on stones and weed stems, as is dulse.

Dulse is a good source of protein and is rich in mineral salts and vitamins. Although it is one of the best known edible seaweeds, it has little flavour and is rather tough. After washing the weed well in cold water, it can be eaten raw and included in salads; in the past it has been given to children to chew instead of chewing gum. It can be dried for later use as a vegetable, or for flavouring sauces, stews and soups, especially fish soup. To cook as a vegetable, the dried weed should be soaked in water for 3 hours and then simmered gently in stock for a further hour until tender and soft. The stock should be strained off and butter and pepper added before serving. Dulse can also be cooked in a similar manner to laver seaweed and made into 'bread': it should be simmered in a little water until mushy, then rolled in oatmeal and finally fried in bacon fat.

Stewed Dulse

2 pints (1200 ml) dulse
¾ pint (450 ml) milk
1 oz (25 g) butter
Salt and pepper

Wash the dulse thoroughly to remove any sand particles. Slice and place in a pan with the milk, butter, salt and pepper and stew until tender for approximately 3½ hours. Serve with brown bread.

Dulse bread

$\frac{1}{2}$ cup chopped dulse
$\frac{1}{2}$ cup oatmeal
2 teaspoons sugar
2 tablespoons yeast
$4\frac{1}{2}$ cups flour
Water

Add the chopped dulse and oatmeal to $1\frac{1}{2}$ cups of boiling water. Stir the mixture, add a teaspoonful of sugar and allow to cool. Add the yeast and a teaspoonful of sugar to $\frac{1}{2}$ cup of warm water and mix with the dulse and oatmeal. Add the flour gradually to the mixture, knead well and then leave the dough in a warm place until it doubles in volume. Knead the dough again, shape into a loaf and leave it to double in size once more. Place in the centre of a moderately hot oven (400°F, gas mark 6) for 15 minutes, then reduce the temperature to 350°F (gas mark 4) for a further 45 minutes when the loaf should be lightly browned.

Dulse sauce

2 tablespoons dulse
2 cups milk or cream

Simmer the chopped dulse in the milk or cream for 20 minutes. The sauce has a sweet tangy taste and is ideal poured over fruit. When made from milk it can also be used as a basis for blancmange.

Dulse soup

1 lb (500 g) fresh dulse
3 oz (75 g) oatmeal
2 pints (1200 ml) water
Salt and pepper

Wash the dulse well and place in a pan with the water. Bring to the boil and simmer for an hour, then strain off the liquid into a pan. Mix the oatmeal with a little water until it has a creamy consistency and stir it slowly into the soup. Allow to boil for a further 10 minutes and add salt and pepper according to taste. The strained-off dulse can be mixed with raw oatmeal, salt and pepper and eaten as a vegetable.

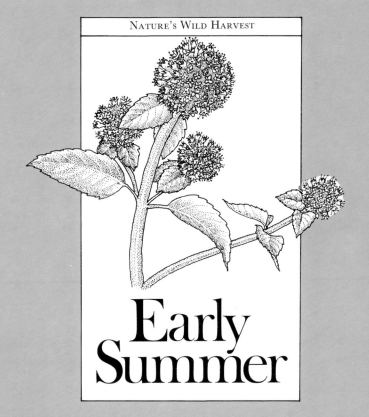

Early Summer

Greater Burdock
Arctium lappa

This rough-looking biennial is of erect habit and often has a stem of 3 to 4 feet (90 to 120 cm) high. A common wasteland plant which also frequents the borders of cultivated fields, it is often mistaken for rhubarb. Its central stem is nodding and bears many side branches. The leaves, which are dull green, rough, downy beneath and stalked, increase in size from about 1 inch (2.5 cm) and oval at the top to extremely large ones at the stem base that are coarsely toothed, 18 inches (45 cm) in length, up to 12 inches (30 cm) wide, and heart-shaped; of our native plants they are only surpassed in size by the butter-bur. The flower-heads, which are in bloom during July and August, appear as many soft purplish spikes arising from a spiky globe-like case (the involucre) which consists of 2 to 3 hundred narrow green bracts each furnished at the end with a tiny upward-turned hook, and delicately webbed from hook to hook.

The purple top of the flower spike is composed of many florets whose corolla tubes are narrow, and have 5 slender lobes above the neck; there is a ring of white filaments enclosing the long petal tube, and from the tube the united heads of the stamens rise as a blackish-purple column; the stamen filaments, however, remain separate. The lower halves of the florets remain encased inside the involucre, and are white in colour. As the fruit matures so the spiky globe increases in size and becomes a formidable burr whose hooks catch onto the coats of passing animals and so are dislodged from the plant and transported. When the burr eventually disintegrates, the seeds are individually dispersed by the wind.

The generic name *Arctium* is from the Greek *arctos*, 'bear', referring to the extremely coarse texture of the hooked bracts comprising the involucres; *lappa* is from the Celtic *llap*, 'a hand', because it catches onto passing animals by its hooks. There is also a lesser burdock, *Arctium minus*, which as its specific name suggests is smaller than *lappa* in many respects.

Burdock contains vitamins A, B and C as well as traces of the elements phosphorus, calcium and iron. The young leaves and the stems are both edible. They should be washed thoroughly, and the stems peeled and cut into 6 cm lengths, before boiling until tender. Alternatively, they can be eaten raw in salads or made into a juice using a blender.

The leaf, root and seed of the burdock are used by herbalists all over the world. The herb is used as a purifying agent for the blood and for skin disorders; the seeds are useful in relieving sciatica and bladder and kidney pains.

Burdock and Dandelion wine

6 oz (150 g) burdock leaves
6 oz (150 g) dandelion leaves
2 lb (1 kg) sugar
7 pints (4 l) water
½ pint (300 ml) white grape concentrate
½ teaspoon tannin
1 teaspoon citric acid
Yeast and nutrient

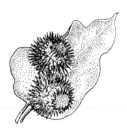

Bring the water to the boil and add the burdock and dandelion leaves. Simmer for 40 minutes and then stir in the sugar until it has completely dissolved. Cover, and allow to cool to room temperature. Then add all the other ingredients, mixing them well into the liquid. Cover again, and keep in a warm place for a week before straining through a nylon sieve into a fermenting jar and fitting an air-lock. Leave to ferment for 2-3 months before racking for the first time, and bottle after about 6 months.

Common Comfrey
Symphytum officinale

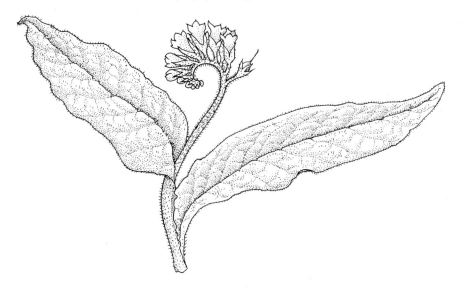

Comfrey is a common herbaceous perennial, particularly along the banks of rivers and other watery habitats. Its brittle roots are fibrous and fleshy, extending in all directions; a feature which makes it difficult to eradicate when overgrown in the garden. The stem is stout, angular, and branched, and it grows from 2 to 3 feet (60 to 90 cm) tall. The leaves are egg-shaped, lanceolate, and narrow below; the large radical leaves are strongly veined and extend down the stem as winged appendages. Both stem and foliage are clothed in bristly hairs, making the plant unpleasant to handle when gathered. The flowers are as clusters of drooping bells, appearing from May to August and in a variety of colours, white, purple, pinkish or greenish. The sepals are narrow or lance-shaped and spreading; they are seemingly more downy in the purple-flowered variety.

Every part of the plant, and especially the roots, contain a copious supply of mucilage; and every part is nutritious, the roots having a sweetish flavour. The leaves, if gathered when young and boiled, provide a pleasing substitute for spinach (the down on the leaves disappears during cooking); or they can be frittered in a batter to form a type of pancake. The root can be boiled as a vegetable, whereas the young shoots, if blanched (forced to grow up through a mound of earth), may be eaten as asparagus, as they are similar in flavour.

The plant also has valuable medicinal qualities and is an important source of allantoin, an outstanding healing agent. If made into a poultice, ointment or lotion, it is most useful in speeding up the re-knitting of fractured bones, and indeed the plant is sometimes called 'knitbone'. It also helps to reduce bruises, swellings and sprains and will heal scars.

A comfrey tea, made by steeping the young leaves in boiling water, helps to relieve symptoms in respiratory illnesses and gastric ulcers. A soothing drink for people suffering from chest diseases can be made by boiling 1 oz (25 g) of the crushed comfrey root in a pint (600 ml) of water for 15 minutes, then adding a pint of milk and simmering for a further quarter of an hour. A glassful of the mixture should be drunk 3 times a day.

Comfrey-leaf fritters

Comfrey leaves
4 oz (100 g) flour
1 egg
Pinch of salt
Milk

Sieve the flour and salt together and beat in the yolk of an egg. Add enough milk to the mixture to create a creamy consistency. Whisk the egg white until stiff and fold into the batter. Wash and dry the comfrey leaves and dip in the batter until well covered. Fry in hot fat until crisp and brown and dust with sugar before serving.

Glasswort or Marsh Samphire
Salicornia europaea

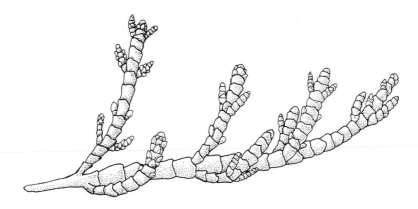

Glasswort is often very abundant on maritime salt marshes and muddy sea shores, and it also occurs on salt marshes inland; it abounds in soda. It is an herbaceous annual growing from 6 to 18 inches (15 to 45 cm), and is very unusual. The stems are bright green and leafless, with compressed divisions, thickening upwards, and notched. They are formed of several fleshy tubes; these are smooth and clear, almost like green glass. In its usual form the habit is erect, but in another (sometimes referred to as *Salicornia procumbens*) the stem is prostrate. The tiny green flowers occur on jointed spikes, each having 8 to 16 flowering segments; at the base of every short segment is a cluster of three flowers. These are all about the same size with the centre one always highest, and occur about $\frac{2}{3}$ of the way up the segment. Each has one or two stamens. Flowers appear during August and September. The name glasswort is derived from its former use in the early manufacture of glass, a use now long superseded.

The plant is at its best for picking in early June. The stem, although stringy, has a salty, juicy flavour. The young shoots can be eaten raw as a tangy addition to salads or served as a vegetable with a knob of butter, after simmering in a little water for 10 minutes. It is sometimes gathered when in flower in August and September and is not quite so tender at this time. However, if the whole plant is cooked slowly in water and served hot with butter, it is still very good to eat. The plant is believed to be an aid to digestion, and in North Lancashire and Norfolk where it is found in abundance it is eaten quite widely.

Wild Gooseberry
Ribes uva-crispa

Woods, copses and hedges seem to be the habitat of this deciduous shrub which grows to heights of 2 to 4 feet (60 to 120 cm). The plant is spreading, with prickly stems and branches, thorns occurring either singly or in twos and threes. Its rounded

3 to 5-lobed leaves unfold in early spring and from the beginning of March the plant is already sending out new growth, its branches winding among the bushes of the hedgerow. In April and on to May the small green flowers are attracting numerous bees, and the foliage by now is very dense. The flowers are drooping and the flower-stalk short and downy. The calyx is bell-shaped with 5 turned-back purplish sepals. The fruit is covered in stiff hairs, unlike the cultivated form which is smooth.

Lancashire gooseberries were regarded as some of the best to be grown in the country and a century ago many well-known varieties were cultivated by ordinary working men, each hoping to gain a prize at the Gooseberry Show for the heaviest gooseberry exhibited. Such old varieties as 'The Jolly Miner', 'Jolly Painter' and 'Lancashire Lad' resulted from their labours. It is reputed that Scottish-grown gooseberries are superior even to the English fruit, for it appears that the flavour increases with the coldness of the climate in which they are grown, provided that there is sufficient warmth for ripening. Pectin, the vegetable jelly of the old chemists, was prepared from this fruit. A sauce made from its berries was once eaten with goose; the plant's common name may have resulted from this. Also, a clear sparkling wine known to countryfolk as 'English champagne' was made from the gooseberry.

Wild gooseberries can be served in the same ways as the cultivated varieties.

Gooseberry jelly

2 lb (1 kg) gooseberries
Sugar
1½ pint (900 ml) water

Wash the gooseberries and place in a pan with the water. Simmer for 1 hour. Strain through a jelly-bag overnight. Measure the liquid and allow 1 lb (500 g) of sugar for each pint (600 ml) of juice. Bring the liquid back to the boil, remove from the heat source and stir in the warmed sugar. When it is dissolved, boil rapidly until the jelly sets when tested (approximately 10 minutes). Skim off the scum and follow the standard procedure.

Gooseberry jam

3 lb (1.5 kg) green gooseberries
3½ lb (1.75 kg) sugar
1 pint (600 ml) water

Top, tail and wash the gooseberries and place in a pan with the water; simmer for 30 minutes, when the fruit should be soft. Add the warmed sugar and stir over a low heat until it is completely dissolved. Boil rapidly until the jam sets when tested (about 10 minutes). Follow the standard procedure as set out in the Introduction.

Gooseberry chutney

4 pints (2.5 l) gooseberries
2 pints (1.2 l) vinegar
2 lb (1 kg) sugar
½ lb (250 g) chopped raisins
2 oz (50 g) mustard seed
1 oz (25 g) ground ginger
4 oz (100 g) salt
2 oz (50 g) chopped onion

Place the gooseberries in the vinegar and bring to the boil. Simmer gently until they are tender. Stir in the sugar until dissolved; allow to cool and mix in the other ingredients. When cold, bottle and seal.

Gooseberry sauce

1 lb (500 g) gooseberries
½ pint (300 ml) water
1 oz (25 g) flour
½ pint (300 ml) milk
1 oz (25 g) butter
½ teaspoon cinnamon
½ teaspoon allspice
1 oz (25 g) brown sugar

Wash, top and tail the gooseberries and place in a pan with the water. Bring to the boil and simmer until tender. Drain off the water and put the gooseberries on one side. Add a quarter of the milk to the flour and blend to a smooth paste with a wooden spoon. Bring the remaining milk to the boil and gradually stir into the flour mixture. Simmer over a low heat for a further 3 minutes, stirring continuously, and then mix in the butter, gooseberries and remaining ingredients.

Gooseberry wine

5 lb (2.5 kg) ripe green gooseberries
2½ lb (1.25 kg) sugar
7 pints (4 l) water
Pectic enzyme
Yeast and nutrient

Crush the berries to a pulp and add the boiling water. Allow to cool to room temperature before adding the pectic enzyme, according to the instructions given on the packet. Cover and leave for 3 days, stirring daily. Strain through a fine nylon sieve and stir in the sugar until it has dissolved completely. Add the yeast and nutrient and pour into a fermenting jar; fit an air-lock. Rack after a few months and again 6 months later. The wine is best drunk after at least a twelve-month period in bottles.

Wild Horseradish
Armoracia rusticana

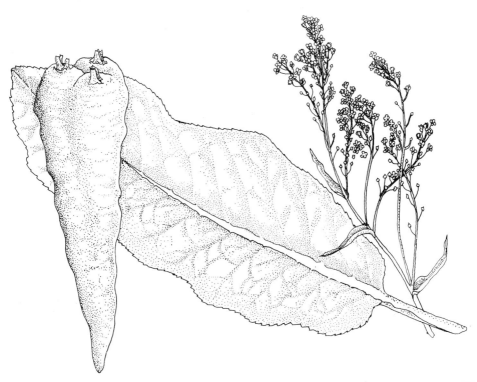

The wild horseradish may be found growing by the side of rivers and streams, in ditches, the corners of fields, and waste places. It often grows as a garden outcast, but at other times it is truly wild. The root-stock is long, stout, cylindrical and tapering. It has a tufted habit and grows from 2 to 3 feet (60 to 90 cm) tall. The radical leaves are heart-shaped or wedge-shaped, have rounded notches at the margin, reticulate veins, and long footstalks. The stem-leaves are long and lanceolate, serrated or entire. The small white flowers appear in May and June, and occur in loose clusters; the petals are four in number and twice the length of the sepals. Its seed pods are borne on long slender stalks but do not ripen in the British Isles. The pouch is shorter than the flowerstalks, ovoid and 4-seeded.

The root of this herbaceous perennial is rich in vitamin C and is normally dug up during the spring. When peeled and grated it can be used as a garnish, but more traditionally as an accompanying sauce for roast beef. Added to cottage cheese and served with salad, it makes a good meal for slimmers. When eaten raw, it has diuretic properties.

Horseradish sauce

2 tablespoons grated horseradish
$\frac{1}{2}$ teaspoon mustard
2 teaspoons white vinegar
1 oz (25 g) flour
$\frac{1}{2}$ pint (300 ml) milk
1 oz (25 g) butter
1 tablespoon cream
Salt and pepper
Pinch of sugar

Add a quarter of the milk to the flour, salt and pepper and blend to a smooth paste with a wooden spoon. Bring the remaining milk to the boil and gradually stir into the flour mixture. Simmer gently, over a low heat, for 3 minutes; stir continuously. Add the butter, horseradish, mustard and vinegar; mix well. Stir in the cream and sugar. Serve cold with roast beef.

Horseradish cream

2 tablespoons grated horseradish
1 tablespoon white vinegar
$\frac{1}{2}$ teaspoon mustard
$\frac{1}{4}$ pint (150 ml) thick cream
Pinch of sugar
Salt and pepper

Whip the cream with the mustard, sugar, salt and pepper. Stir in the horseradish and vinegar. Chill before serving.

Horseradish vinegar

1 large root horseradish
1 onion
1 pint (600 ml) malt vinegar

Wash and peel the horseradish root and then shred it. Fill jars with the root and chopped onion until they are one-third full; top them up with hot vinegar. Leave the jars to cool; cover, shake thoroughly and allow to stand in a warm place for 6 weeks, shaking now and again. When this time has elapsed, taste the vinegar and, if there is sufficient flavour, strain and rebottle it ready for use. Otherwise, leave it for a few more weeks.

Horseradish vinegar is best served with fatty meat and oily fish.

Common Mallow
Malva sylvestris

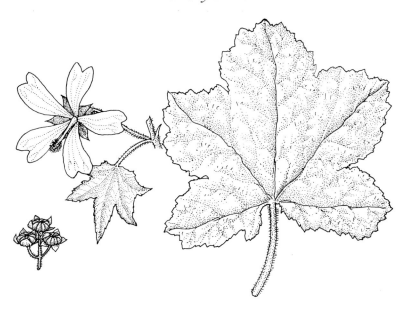

This perennial, deciduous, herbaceous and sand-loving plant quite often grows to a height of 4 feet (120 cm), and can be met with along country roadsides, on waste pieces of ground or the borders of fields and the like. The stem is erect, branched and woody; the leaves are longstalked and have 3 to 7 lobes. The lower leaves are kidney-shaped. The upper surface is smooth, and the lower surface covered with rough hairs as are the stem and leaf-stalks. Those familiar lilac flowers with veins of a purplish tint are in bloom from June to August. The 5 petals are narrow at the base but broader at the top and with a deep central cleft. The 5 sepals are much shorter than the petals. Looking into the flower from above, the sepals appear between the gaps in the petals like a 5-rayed green star.

Country children know the fruit of the mallow well, and often call the plant 'Cheese-cake', 'Cheese-log' or 'Cheese-flower', for it resembles a tiny flattened round Dutch Cheese, and is composed of a dozen or more segments, rather like a peeled tangerine, each segment containing a single curved seed. It is sometimes erroneously referred to by country folk as 'Marsh Mallow' which is possibly a corruption of 'Mash Mallow' since its leaves were employed in fomentations. The specific name *sylvestris* suggests that the plant should frequent a woodland habitat.

Common mallow contains the vitamins A, B_1, B_2 and C, and both the leaves and the seeds are edible. The young leaves can be eaten raw and chopped in salads; the older leaves should be cooked like spinach and eaten either as a vegetable or mixed with boiled rice, and are glutinous enough to add to casseroles and soups. Before eating, the hairy leaves should be washed well as they tend to collect dust particles. Mallow seeds have a mildly nutty flavour and country children still pick and nibble them in certain districts.

Mallow is beneficial in the treatment of painful swellings and is used as a digestive and diuretic herb, as well as in the making of an external lotion for acne. The leaves have the reputation of easing the pain of a wasp sting if rubbed on the affected area. A certain cure for a cold was believed to be bathing the feet in a decoction of the leaves, flowers and roots.

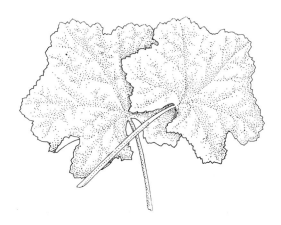

Mallow soup

1 lb (500 g) mallow leaves
2 pints (1200 ml) stock
2 teaspoons cooking oil
2 crushed cloves garlic
2 teaspoons ground coriander
Salt and pepper

Remove the stalks from the leaves and discard. Chop the leaves and simmer in the stock for 10 minutes. Gently fry the crushed cloves of garlic, coriander, salt and pepper in the oil. Stir in the stock mixture and simmer for a further 5 minutes. Serve hot.

Marjoram
Origanum vulgare

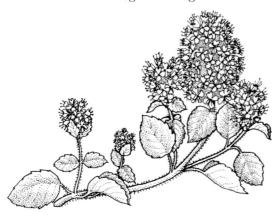

Chalky hillside pastures, tall cliffs, upland districts in woods and copses, or even hedgerows where the soil is dry or covered with small fragmented rubble, all provide a suitable habitat for this deciduous, herbaceous perennial. Marjoram grows to heights of 1 to 2 feet (30 to 60 cm). The slender stems are erect, quadrangular, purple, downy and branched, emanating from a woody, creeping root. The 1 inch (2.5 cm) long, egg-shaped leaves are stalked and opposite, toothed, and downy beneath. The kind of flowers produced varies; in some plants they are of a richer purple and somewhat larger than those of others, but they are always borne in dense compact heads with purple egg-shaped bracts which are longer than, and beneath, the calyx. In the larger, complete or perfect flowers, with both male and female organs present, the tube of the corolla is 7 mm long. The smaller, fainter-coloured flowers are incomplete females with no stamens present, and the tube is only 4 to 5 mm long; they are, however, in bloom a week before the perfect ones. This sweet-smelling plant is in flower from June through to October (mainly July to August). *Origanum* is from the Greek *oros*, 'hill', and *ganos*, 'joy'; hence it is some-times given the name 'Joy of the Mountain'. The Latin specific name *vulgare* sug-gests the plant to be of common occurrence whereas it is really somewhat local.

To dry the herb, cut off the stems at ground level, tie together and hang in a dry place at a temperature of no more than 38°C (100°F). The leaves when crisp can be crushed and stored in airtight containers. The herb provides an excellent flavouring for all meats, stews, soups and casseroles; traditionally, however, it is used with lamb. It can also be sprinkled over chops and steaks or mixed with stuffings.

Marjoram tea, made by pouring a pint (600 ml) of boiling water over a heaped tablespoonful of the dried herb and left to infuse for a few minutes, is said to be good for cases of stomach weakness and breast troubles. In ancient times, the plant was valued for the treatment of narcotic poisoning and convulsions. It was also used to allay toothache and rheumatic pains and is said to be a good remedy for falling hair.

Meadowsweet
Filipendula ulmaria

This is a sweet-scented perennial growing from 2 to 3 feet, even 4 feet (60 to 90 cm, even 120 cm) tall. It thrives in damp situations, being quite common growing along riversides and hollows in moist meadowland on a clay soil; but is also found on sandy loam. The stem is erect, reddish-tinted, furrowed and angular, it may be simple or branched. Even the gentlest breeze causes the leaves to quiver thus revealing their whitish underside which is covered in a soft down, the upper surface being deep green. The terminal leaflets are large, palmately lobed into a number of pointed segments (3 to 5), and toothed. Their resemblance in shape to the leaves of the elm tree (*Ulmus*) is responsible for the specific name *ulmaria*. From late May until early October their waving plumes of creamy-white, almond-scented flowers rise clear above all others in the waterside meadows and along the edges of brooks and streams.

A very old recipe says that if the flowers are infused in liquor of any kind this results in a pleasant taste, and it also recommends adding them to mead. An almond flavouring is detected if a few unopened buds are placed in the mouth; the same taste is also present in the roots which if dried, ground and mixed with meal make a good substitute for flour.

Meadowsweet has also been called Queen of the Meadow (from its old name *Regina prati*) and Bridewort from the days when it was used for strewing houses at wedding festivals, and because of its resemblance to the white plumes of feathers once worn by brides.

The sweet scent of the flowers has caused them to be used in a similar way to lavender. The flowers, either fresh or dried, can be placed in wardrobes and linen cupboards to give a pleasant perfume.

Meadowsweet tea, made from the leaves and flowers of the plant, is a good remedy for mild indigestion, dropsy and children's diarrhoea. The tea is made by pouring ¾ pint (450 ml) of boiling water over an ounce (25 g) of fresh or dried flowers. It should be left to stand for 3-4 minutes and then strained before drinking.

Meadowsweet wine

7 pints (4 l) flower heads
3 lb (1.5 kg) sugar
7 pints (4 l) water
½ pint (300 ml) white grape concentrate
1 teaspoon grape tannin
Juice of 2 lemons
Yeast and nutrient

Add boiling water to the flowers and stir in the lemon juice, grape concentrate and sugar. Allow to cool to room temperature before adding the tannin, yeast and nutrient. Cover well and leave to ferment for 8-10 days in a warm place, stirring daily. Strain into a fermenting jar and fit an air-lock. Rack for the first time when the wine clears and bottle a few months later.

Pig-nut or Earth Nut
Conopodium majus

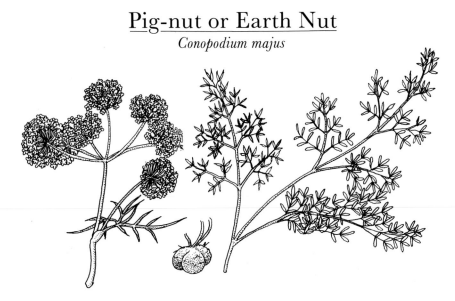

The pig-nut can be found growing in sandy and gravelly pastureland, in fields and meadows, grass verges by the roadside, and woods. This herbaceous perennial is erect in habit, usually growing to a height of about 18 inches (45 cm); the stem is simple, slender and rounded, emanating from a small tuber about the size of a hazelnut. The lower leaves are on long stalks and are tri-ternate (having three leaflets that are trebly divided); the stem leaves are few in number and almost sessile, deeply divided practically to the base, and with linear segments. Its tiny flowers are borne in wide terminal umbels, and occur during May and June; there are no bracts or bracteoles. The fruit is narrowly egg-shaped with several vittae (oil stripes).

The tubers of the pig-nut are sweet and edible, and they are eagerly sought after and uprooted by pigs—hence the common name. In times of famine they have provided a nutritious food for man, with a high farinaceous content. Country children often dig up the nut-like tubers and eat them in an uncooked condition; they have a taste very similar in flavour to the sweet chestnut. In days gone by the powdered roots were recommended as a cough remedy.

Wild Raspberry
Rubus idaeus

The wild raspberry is a perennial shrub of some 3 to 6 feet (1 to 2 metres) in height, whose stem is erect and woody, furnished with a great many prickles and producing numerous suckers. The habitat is heaths, woods and thickets, quite often in wettish areas. Its leaves are pinnate with 3 to 5 coarsely toothed leaflets, egg-shaped with a long point, and downy white on the underside. The flowers, which appear from late May and June through to August, are corymbose and drooping, axillary and terminal; they have short white petals which are only equal in length to the sepals. From early July the drupes ripen to red or amber and fall to the ground if not picked. The wild raspberry seems to be quite common in North Wales especially in the neighbourhood of Betws-y-coed; in some northern counties it occurs not infrequently in rocky woods.

Botanists have named over 100 species of wild raspberry occurring in Britain, which we do not propose to treat individually, but would mention *R. mucronotoides*, listed as a Scottish plant, and *R. cariensis*, which is said to be locally abundant in the west, especially in North Devon. In Sweden it appears to be most luxuriant in those forests where fires have been lit, seeming to thrive among wood ashes and cinders. The raspberry is a native of most European countries: it is the *Framboisier* of the French, the *Himbeerstrauch* of the Germans, the *Braamboos* of the Dutch, the *Rovo ideo* of the Italians, the *Zara idea* of the Spaniards, and *Malinik* of the Russians. Our forefathers called the fruit *Raspis* or Hindberry.

Raspberries are one of the first soft fruits to ripen, usually in early July. They can be eaten raw when fresh, stored away in the freezer for later use, or made into jam or jelly. They also make a tasty stuffing for game birds.

A herbal tea made from the dried young leaves acts as a tonic to the uterine muscles of pregnant women, and when drunk 3 times a day in the last few weeks of pregnancy is said to quicken the birth of the baby. In years gone by the raspberry was used in many home remedies such as cough mixtures and ointments, and raspberry vinegar is one such remedy which has been passed down from generation to generation.

Raspberry jelly

3 lb (1.5 kg) raspberries
1 cup water
Sugar
Juice of 1 lemon

Place the raspberries with the water in a preserving pan and simmer gently until the fruit is soft and mushy. Strain through a jelly-bag overnight. Measure the liquid and allow 1 pound (500 g) of sugar for each pint. Re-heat the liquid and stir in the warmed sugar and lemon juice, but over a low heat; ensure that all has dissolved. Boil rapidly until the jelly sets when tested. Follow the standard procedure on jelly-making.

Raspberry jam

3 lb (1.5 kg) raspberries
3 lb (1.5 kg) sugar
Juice of 1 lemon

Simmer the raspberries in their own juice for 15 minutes. Add the lemon juice and warmed sugar and stir until dissolved. Boil rapidly until the jam sets when tested. Follow the standard procedure.

Gooseberry
Ribes uva-crispa

Yarrow
Achillea millefolium

Woodruff
Galium odoratum

Wild Strawberry
Fragaria vesca

Comfrey
Symphytum officinale

Honeysuckle
Lonicera periclymenum

Burdock
Arctium lappa

Glasswort
Salicornia europaea

Elderflowers
Sambucus nigra

Meadowsweet
Filipendula ulmaria

Lime
Tilia vulgaris

Horseradish
Armoracia rusticana

Common Mallow
Malva sylvestris

Marjoram
Origanum vulgare

Water Mint
Mentha aquatica

Watercress
Nasturtium officinale

Wild Raspberry
Rubus idaeus

Raspberry wine

4 lb (2 kg) raspberries
3 lb (1.5 kg) sugar
7 pints (4 l) water
Pectic enzyme
Yeast and nutrient

Pour the boiling water over the crushed fruit and allow to cool. Add the enzyme, cover well, and leave for 3-4 days, stirring daily. Strain through a fine nylon sieve onto the sugar and stir until it has all dissolved. Add the yeast and nutrient and leave covered for a day in a warm place. Pour the liquid into a fermenting jar and fit an air-lock. Rack when the wine clears and again a few months later before bottling.

Raspberry fool

1 lb (500 g) raspberries
¼ pint (150 ml) water
Juice of 1 lemon
¼ pint (150 ml) custard
1 oz (25 g) sugar
¼ pint (150 ml) cream

Place the raspberries, water and lemon juice in a pan and simmer until soft. Rub through a sieve and stir in the sugar and custard. Whip the cream until thick and fold into the raspberry mixture. Chill before serving.

Wild Strawberry

Fragaria vesca

The wild strawberry is a much smaller plant than the cultivated type and rarely more than 8 inches (20 cm) in height. This shade-loving plant is often found growing along banks that are overgrown by trees or tall vegetation. It may also be found growing quite profusely in woodland glades, where it enjoys a uniform but not too abundant supply of moisture and a diffusion of light and sunshine. Although it is primarily a sand-loving plant requiring a fair amount of humus, it may also be found growing in rocky soil. Its leaves are trifoliate, sessile and toothed on the margin, and like the flower-stalks are clothed in silky hairs. The 'stolons' or runners are 1 foot (30 cm) or more in length. Late April and May are perhaps the main flowering months, but flowers can occur throughout the entire summer, so it is not unusual to find both ripe fruit and flowers together on the same plant. The white flowers are small and delicate with 5 white petals and an outer cup of 5 green sepals. In the centre there are numerous fragile stamens arranged around a small green mound; on the mound are many tiny green carpels each of which contains a seed. It is similar in pattern to the rose but with one major difference: in the centre of the rose is a hollow in which the carpels lie. Both the mound of the strawberry and the depression of the rose are the end of the flower stalk. So the strawberry is also a 'false fruit', the true fruits being the small hard yellow bodies that lie adhered to and distributed over its fleshy surface.

It is also referred to as the hedge strawberry. The wild fruit is very small but it is agreed by many experts that even the finest cultivated strawberry cannot boast a better flavour. They are perfect when eaten as soon after picking as possible, served with cream.

A herbal tea can be made by pouring 1 pint (600 ml) of boiling water over a handful of fresh or dried young leaves and infusing for 4 minutes before straining. This provides a good tonic for convalescents and sufferers of upset stomachs. The runners or stolons were once used in medicine in a preparation for wounds. Eating the fruit in sufficient quantities has been considered a cure for all manner of ills.

Woodruff
Galium odoratum

This humus-loving, herbaceous perennial is almost exclusively a woodland species, growing in the shaded conditions afforded by thickly-clustered trees. In certain parts of Kent the plant covers large areas in the woodlands; growing with it we often find Wood Sorrel, Sweet Violet or Primrose. The stem is erect and seldom over 1 foot (30 cm) tall, and is more or less simple, square, and smooth but furrowed. The leaves are green, lanceolate and arranged in whorls, the lower whorls containing 2 to 6 leaves, the upper ones 6 to 9 leaves. The margins are rough with forward-pointing prickles; they are light-sensitive, turning yellow if exposed to strong daylight. In May and on to June one can detect a sweet scent of newly-mown hay in the woodlands; this comes from the woodruff's attractive little white flowers that are borne in terminal corymbs (each flower rising to the same level). Collectively they are conspicuous; they are devoid of leaves. The fruits are like rough little balls, thickly covered in hooked bristles which catch in the wool of passing animals and are thus dispersed. Its specific name *odoratum* is Latin and refers to the plant's smell. The leaves of woodruff were once used in the household, being laid amongst linen and cloths, not only to impart their sweet odour (which they retain for several years), but also as a repellent to moths. Ladies often used it as a filling for ornamental scent-bags. It has also been called Sweet Grass, Hay Plant, and Star Grass (because of its whorled leaves).

The plant should be picked just before flowering; it has been used in the making of wines, champagne, brandy and vodka. Woodruff tea, made from the fresh or dried leaves and flowers, makes a good substitute for ordinary tea and, medicinally, is said to promote perspiration and ease liver complaints. To prepare, pour 1 pint (600 ml) of boiling water over a handful of leaves and flowers and allow to stand for 4 minutes before straining.

Yarrow or Milfoil
Achillea millefolium

This common, deciduous, herbaceous perennial is very much at home on sandy soils, especially in dry pastureland, along the roadside, or on waste grounds. It grows between 1 and 2 feet (30 and 60 cm) tall, the stem is rigid and erect, prostrate below, and angular. The bottom of the stem is covered in thick down. The leaves are fern-like with many leaflets, which when young are folded face to face, and each leaflet has lobes on either side of the stalk. These are again cut into slender acute segments, and lightly covered with silky grey hairs. The main leaf rib is a whitish channel with a border of dark green. The radical leaves are stalked. Flowering occurs from June to September, when the hitherto tight clusters of dull grey buds, having shed their covering of white hairs, begin to open, revealing numerous white flowers each usually with 5 marginal florets, and borne in a flat terminal corymb. On close inspection we find that the yellow centre of the flowers is composed of 20 smaller florets. The fruit which is flat and margined is adapted for wind dispersal but has no pappus (a tuft of down is often present on the seeds of composite plants).

The generic name *Achillea* is named after Achilles who is credited with being the first to discover that the plant healed wounds; *millefolium* is from the Latin *mille* a thousand, and *folium* a leaf; alluding to the numerous divisions of the leaf.

Yarrow leaves have a tangy, peppery taste, and add flavour when chopped raw in salads. They can also be boiled to make a green vegetable. The flowers have a strong nutty perfume and are used with the young leaves to make an excellent tea. The flowers and leaves should be dried at no more than 38°C (100°F) or they can be used fresh. To make the tea, pour 1 pint (600 ml) over 1 ounce (25 g) of the herb; let it stand for a few minutes, then drain off the liquid. A wineglassful should be drunk at intervals during the day. The tea is a good remedy for the common cold as it produces perspiration and opens the pores of the skin. It is also a digestive tonic and acts as a blood purifier.

Pungent juices lie within the leaf tissues and to chew the leaves was a supposed cure for toothache. In past times, the leaves were picked, rolled up and inserted up the nostrils to cure headaches due to congestion in the head; they were even supposed to stop nosebleeds. The plant was also used to make an ointment, by Icelanders and Highlanders, which was used to heal wounds quickly. Some people have even found it to be a good hair restorer.

Yarrow wine

1 gallon (4.5 l) yarrow leaves and flowers
½ pint (300 ml) white grape concentrate
2 lb (1 kg) sugar
½ teaspoon grape tannin
7 pints (4 l) water
Juice of 2 lemons
Yeast and nutrient

Pour the boiling water onto the flowers and leaves. Cover and allow to cool to room temperature. Stir in the grape concentrate and juice of both lemons and leave covered for 24 hours. Bring briefly to the boil whilst stirring in the sugar, and after it has cooled again to room temperature add the tannin, yeast and nutrient. Leave covered for a week in a warm place, stirring daily, before straining into a fermenting jar and fitting an air-lock. Rack when the wine clears and bottle after about 6 months.

Watercress
Nasturtium officinale

This is a widely distributed, water-loving, herbaceous perennial that grows most luxuriantly in shallow running water. Its long, wavy, hollow stems float on the surface, and only become erect or semi-erect where the flower stems rise clear of the water. At other times it can be found growing in ditches, ponds or pools, and even in the damp mud at the water's edge. Watercress is a large plant, often reaching 4 feet (120 cm) in length. Its leaves are perhaps the best means of identification—they are pinnate, with egg-shaped or oval leaflets on each side of a common stem, lobed, slightly toothed, and almost heart-shaped at the base. After much exposure to the light they acquire a purplish-brown tint. Flowering commences during May and continues into August. The small flowers are white, often turning purple with age. Their petals are twice the length of the calyx and the flowers are easily overlooked. The seed pods are longer than the flower-stalks and open from below upwards; the seeds which are flattened lengthwise are arranged in two rows.

Watercress is sometimes referred to as 'Brooklime' or 'Brown Cress' and was probably first cultivated in England right at the beginning of the nineteenth century and was one of the first green vegetables to be eaten regularly in Europe. The wild plant

is identical to the commercially-grown variety. It requires a regular flow of clean water and should never be picked from stagnant ponds or streams which run through sheep pasture, because the eggs of the liverfluke are then more likely to be found in the plant's hollow stems. The older mature shoots, on which the leaves have a bronze tint, should be picked for eating; they are much tastier than the younger shoots without becoming tough. Watercress is rich in vitamins A, C and E and also has a high protein content. The sprigs should be washed thoroughly and are splendid in salads or as sandwich fillers. They can also be boiled like spinach as a green vegetable or used in soups, but the vitamin content will be reduced.

Medicinally, watercress was used by earlier civilizations as an anti-scorbutic (preventing scurvy), and it was once thought capable of removing warts if the leaves were laid upon them.

Watercress soup

2 pints (1.2 l) watercress
2 onions
1 oz (25 g) butter
1½ pints (900 ml) chicken stock
Marjoram
Salt and pepper

Chop the onions and fry gently in the butter until soft. Add the watercress and cook for a few minutes. Add the chicken stock, marjoram, salt and pepper and bring to the boil. Blend the mixture in a liquidizer, then reheat before serving.

Water Mint or Water Capitate Mint
Mentha aquatica

Water mint is a common deciduous, herbaceous perennial whose luxuriant growth fringes such moist habitats as riversides, pools and ditches; it also frequents marshland and other boggy areas. It grows in peaty and clay soils. The stem is erect, reaching heights of 1½ to 2 feet (45 to 60 cm), square, and covered in rough hairs; it produces stolons (runners) with creeping roots. The uppermost leaves are smaller than the flowers and serve as bracts; the lower ones are egg-shaped (heart-shaped at the base), and stalked, roughly haired, and serrated. It blooms from July to September, having pale bluish-lilac flowers growing in dense axillary whorls. The highest flowers form a globular terminal head. The stalks carry hairs that are somewhat bent backwards. The small flowered plants are female, and far less plentiful than the larger hermaphroditic ones. Every part of the plant emits that familiar strong and rather unpleasant odour. Water mint is the most common of all the mints. In the Hebrides it has been used as a repellent of mice, with bunches of the plant being placed amongst wheatsheaves to deter this rodent from damaging the wheat. It was also equally successful against mice when placed in food stores.

The generic name *Mentha* is from the Greek *mintha* or *minthe*. Mintha, a nymph, was transformed into this plant by Prosperine. The specific name *aquatica* refers to the watery habitat in which it grows. Its strong smell and taste is that of peppermint, and an oil is extracted from this and other members of the genus to manufacture oil of peppermint.

Pick the leaves when they are at their best and strip them from their stalks for drying or freezing. A mint tea can be made by pouring ¾ pint (450 ml) of boiling water over fresh or dried leaves. After straining, serve with a slice of lemon or orange and sweeten with honey. A wineglass of unsweetened mint tea is a good remedy for nausea and morning sickness.

Honeysuckle
Lonicera periclymenum

Woodbine was an old name given to this deciduous shrub, because of its habit of embracing or climbing over other plants. It likes the darker parts of woodlands and copses where it seeks support from a nearby sapling or an old tree. We can also find it along the hedgerows and by the roadside, clinging to overhanging branches of blackthorn, hawthorn or holly, twining round their stems in a clockwise direction as it follows the sun from east to west. Its hold becomes closer and tighter as the stem of the host plant grows in circumference. It likes a sandy-loam or a clay soil with an abundance of humus. The honeysuckle may attain lengths of up to 20 feet (6 metres). The leaves often appear early in March; they are all distinct and not joined at the base, egg-shaped, stalkless above, and with short stalks below, sometimes downy beneath.

It flowers from May to July. At first the deep creamy, closely set buds are erect, each tube about 1 inch (25 mm) long, becoming crimson tinted and thicker towards the tip. Those buds that are to open that day do so at around 7 p.m., giving off a strong but fragrant odour as the lobes of the corolla begin to curl backwards, and soon assuming a horizontal position. The night-flying hawk moths are quickly attracted, their very long proboscides well adapted to reach the honey deep down inside the long tube. The flowers are carried in long-stalked, terminal whorls, their mouths agape with 5 long stamens projecting, which on loosing their pollen turn downwards making way for the stigma to rise. As the old flowers fall so the berries begin to develop, ripening from green to a semi-transparent vivid scarlet. They are about the size of a pea, and juicy.

The generic name *Lonicera* was given in memory of the sixteenth-century German botanist Adam Lonicer, and *periclymenum* was the Greek name for Honeysuckle or a similar plant. The common name honeysuckle comes from the Anglo-Saxon *hunig-suge*. Other common names include Eglantine, Caprifole and Lady's Fingers. Perfumers make fragrant essences and waters from the honeysuckle's flowers.

Medicinally, the flowers have also been used by herbalists to treat respiratory disorders and asthma. A decoction of the leaves acts as a laxative and has been used beneficially in liver diseases. However, the berries should not be eaten as they are poisonous. A fine wine may be brewed from the flower heads as follows.

Honeysuckle wine

3 pints (1.75 l) honeysuckle blossom
3 lb (1.5 kg) sugar
$\frac{1}{4}$ pint (150 ml) white grape concentrate
7 pints (4 l) water
2 lemons
1 teaspoon grape tannin
Yeast and nutrient
1 Campden tablet

Pick the flowers on a dry, sunny day, when they are fully open, and wash them. Add the cold water and 2 lb (1 kg) of the sugar to the flowers, stirring until the sugar has dissolved. Mix in the grape concentrate and the juice from both lemons, together with a crushed Campden tablet. Leave for 24 hours before adding the grape tannin, yeast and nutrient. Ferment in a warm place for 6–8 days, stirring occasionally. Then dissolve the remaining sugar in the liquid before straining it through a fine nylon sieve into a fermenting jar; fit an air-lock. Rack when the wine clears, and then again a few months later just before bottling.

Common Elder or Bourtree
Sambucus nigra

The elder is a common deciduous bush of irregular, even straggling growth, and with many stems emanating from a common base. It will grow in almost any situation but thrives on a well-drained but moist substrate, with a high nitrogen content; occasionally it attains tree proportions on a rich soil. The creamy-white bisexual flowers are in evidence during June and July, each flower is $\frac{1}{5}$ inch (5 mm) across and occurring terminally in flat-topped clusters on five radiating main stalks. These flower clusters are usually about 6 inches (15 cm) in diameter, but inflorescences of twice this size are often recorded. The elderberries develop quickly, ripening from green to purplish-black drupes by late August and September. The leaves are ovate with a dentate margin, are arranged in pairs on opposite sides of a common stem, and have a terminal leaflet. The deeply fissured, greyish-brown bark is often seen to have cracked and broken away from the trunk and branches. Herbalists have long known the medicinal values of the elder with all parts of the tree being used at some time.

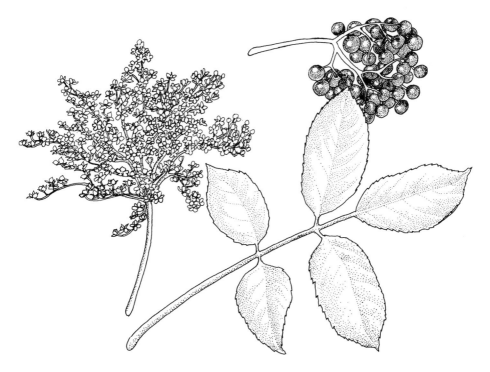

Elderflower and Gooseberry jelly

6 lb (3 kg) green gooseberries
4 large elderflowers
1½ pints (900 ml) water
Sugar

Wash, top and tail the gooseberries and place in a pan with the water. Simmer until soft and pulpy, then strain through a jelly-bag overnight. Measure the juice, allowing 1 pound (500 g) of sugar for each pint (600 ml) of liquid. Reheat the juice and add the warmed sugar, stirring until dissolved. Tie the elderflowers in a piece of muslin and place in the juice. Boil rapidly until the jelly sets when tested. Remove the flowers and follow the standard procedure.

Elderflower vinegar

Elderflower clusters
White wine vinegar

Pick the elderflowers when they are fully open and check to remove any insects. Remove the flowers from the stalks and place them in jars. Pack them well down, and when half full top up with the vinegar. Allow to stand in a warm place for 2 weeks or until the vinegar is sufficiently flavoured for your own taste; then strain through a jelly-bag. Bottle and seal the vinegar and store in a dry place. It can be used in the making of sauces and salad dressings.

Elderflower fritters

Elderflower clusters
4 oz (100 g) flour
1 egg
Pinch of salt
Milk

Sieve the salt and flour together and beat in the yolk of an egg. Add enough milk to the mixture to make a creamy consistency. Whisk the egg white until stiff and fold into the batter. Wash and dry the elderflower clusters, and check all insects have been removed. Dip them in the batter until well-covered and fry in hot fat until crisp and brown. Serve the fritters hot, dusted with sugar.

Elderflower wine

1 pint (600 ml) flower tips
3 lb (1.5 kg) sugar
$\frac{1}{4}$ pint (150 ml) white grape concentrate
7 pints (4 l) water
1 teaspoon grape tannin
3 lemons
Yeast and nutrient

The flowers should be picked on a sunny day so that they are fully open. Remove them from their stems by trimming with a pair of scissors, until a pint (600 ml) is obtained. Boil the water and pour onto the flowers, adding the sugar, concentrate and lemon juice. When the mixture has cooled to room temperature, add the grape tannin, yeast and nutrient. Leave covered in a warm place for 5 days before straining through nylon into a fermenting jar. Fit an air-lock and leave to ferment. Rack for the first time when the wine clears and again 6 weeks later just before bottling.

Elderflower and Gooseberry jam

4 lb (2 kg) green gooseberries
6 large elderflowers
4 lb (2 kg) sugar
1 pint (600 ml) water

Wash, top and tail the gooseberries and place in a pan with the water. Simmer until the gooseberries are soft but not pulpy. Add the warmed sugar and stir until dissolved. Tie the elderflowers in a piece of muslin and place in the pan. Boil rapidly until the jam sets when tested. Remove the flowers and follow the normal procedure.

Common Lime or Linden
Tilia vulgaris

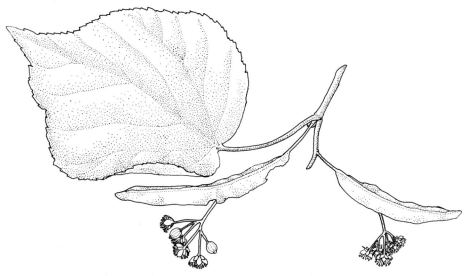

The common lime is deciduous, and is a natural hybrid between the small-leaved and the large-leaved limes. It shows a preference for rich fertile sandy soils but will also thrive on rock soil. Quite often it reaches heights of 50 feet (17 metres), and under exceptional circumstances 120 feet (37 metres) or even more. The spreading branches hang downwards at their extremities. Its leaves unfold during April and May. At first they are thin and membranous, light green, hairless, and translucent; later they become darker and of a coarse texture. The outline is heart-shaped but with a short, abrupt point, and a serrated margin. The leaf is twice the length of the leaf-stalk. From June to July and into August the lime produces pendulous cymes of bisexual flowers, each cyme consists of some 4 to 10 pale whitish-green, sweet-scented flowers, and has a lance-shaped leaf-like bract growing from the base of the long flower-stalk. There are 5 green deciduous sepals, 5 yellowish petals, and numerous free or united stamens which shed their pollen before the stigma is mature, thus eliminating the possibility of self-pollination. The fruit is a single-celled, downy but leathery, thick-walled nutlet about $\frac{1}{3}$ of an inch (8 mm) in diameter, and faintly ribbed.

The small-leaved lime, as its name implies, usually has smaller leaves than the common lime. These are about 2 inches (5 cm) across, smooth above, but the underside has patches of brown hairs in the vein axils. Its fruit is thin-shelled, brittle and not ribbed, or scarcely ever so. As one would expect, the large-leaved lime usually has larger leaves than the common lime. They are about 4 inches (10 cm) long, rougher, and the underside is downy. Each cyme bears 3 flowers. When ripe the oval woody fruit is strongly ribbed. Limes are often planted by the roadside and seem well able to withstand excessive pruning and pollarding. Its wood was formerly used in carving and examples may be seen in St. Paul's, and Trinity College Library at Cambridge. Honey made by bees visiting the Lime is said to be one of the best. *Tilia* is the Latin name for the lime tree, and *vulgaris* refers to its common occurrence throughout temperate Europe and the British Isles. The word lime is a variant of the old English *lind*.

The young leaves can be eaten in salads or used as a sandwich filling. The pale flowers make an excellent herbal tea. They should be picked on a warm dry day in June or July, just as they begin to open, and then carefully taken home and dried. To make the tea, pour $\frac{3}{4}$ pint (450 ml) of boiling water over a heaped tablespoon of the dried flowers and infuse for 3 or 4 minutes before straining. It makes a useful bedtime drink for it has been used as a mild sedative; in France, it is given to over-tired or teething babies. It is also good for nervous indigestion and reducing fevers and was once prescribed as a treatment for chronic epilepsy.

Limeflower wine

4 pints (2.5 l) limeflowers
7 pints (4 l) water
$\frac{1}{2}$ pint (300 ml) white grape concentrate
2 lb (1 kg) sugar
1 teaspoon citric acid
$\frac{1}{2}$ teaspoon wine tannin
Yeast and nutrient

Bring the water to the boil and allow to cool to room temperature. Add the lime-flowers, citric acid and grape concentrate and leave covered in a warm place for a day. Bring back to the boil, stir in the sugar until it has dissolved and allow to cool again to room temperature. Add the yeast, nutrient and tannin. Cover and leave in a warm place for a week, stirring twice daily. Strain through nylon netting into a fermenting jar and fit an air-lock. Rack when the wine clears and bottle after 6 months.

Late Summer

Wild Angelica
Angelica sylvestris

A humus-loving, deciduous, herbaceous perennial with an erect habit and requiring continual moisture and shade, wild angelica can be found in low lying woodlands, in marshes, along the borders of rivers or streams, and even in moist mountainous regions if the conditions are suitably humid. The plant often attain heights of 5 to 6 feet (1.5 to 2 metres), but 8 to 10 feet ($2\frac{1}{2}$ to 3 metres) has been recorded. Its tall, stout stem is 1 to 2 inches (25 to 50 mm) in diameter, green or purplish in colour, rather downy near the umbels but otherwise mostly hairless; it is furrowed and hollow. In outline the leaves are triangularly ternate. The large leaflets are egg-shaped (often heart-shaped at the base), evenly serrated, stalked, and not running down the stem. The sheaths are large. Its small pinkish-white flowers are numerous, and in large terminal umbels with 30 to 40 rays; the petals are slightly hooded; the calyx-lobes are small or lacking. Flowering occurs from June to August. The fruit is small, egg-shaped, flattened and margined, and is readily dispersed by the wind or dislodged by passing animals or humans.

Country folk knew it as Ait-skeiters ('oat-shooters') because their children would shoot oats through its hollow stem in the manner of a pea-shooter. It has also been called Trumpet Keck, because boys used to fashion its hollow stems into crude trumpets. *Angelica* is Latin for 'angelic', which alludes to the plant's supposed magical properties; *sylvestris* refers to its woodland habitat.

Do not confuse angelica with hemlock (*Conium maculatum*).

Angelica has a tangy, slightly bitter taste, similar to that of Juniper berries. The stem is the part of the plant most used and should be picked in April or May. It can be candied with sugar and eaten as a sweet (see recipe below), or added to fruits when cooking to reduce their tartness.

The seeds, which should be picked in August and September, are used in producing drinks such as Vermouth and Chartreuse. The plant has been used in toilet-water preparation, in the manufacture of a yellow dye and as a cure for dog bites.

It is a medicinal herb which is said to aid digestion, cleanse the blood and stimulate the kidneys. A tea, made by infusing an ounce (25 g) of the herb with a pint (600 ml) of boiling water is a useful tonic which helps to dispel 'wind'. Its taste is not unlike that of China tea.

Candied Angelica

Angelica stems
1 lb (500 g) castor sugar
1 teacup water

Wash and dry the angelica stems and cut them into lengths of about 2 inches (5 cm). Dissolve the castor sugar in the water and bring the mixture to the boil slowly. Measure the temperature of the sugar mixture with a sweet thermometer and when it reaches 115°C (240°F) allow it to boil for a further minute. Add a few of the angelica stems to the syrup, leave for one minute, then remove and place on kitchen foil to cool. Repeat this process for all the stems. When the stems have cooled, place them with the foil into a preheated oven which has been turned off, and allow them to dry.

Angelica liqueur

1 oz (25 g) fresh angelica stem
1 oz (25 g) bitter almonds
1¾ pints (1 l) brandy
1 pint (600 ml) syrup made from white sugar

Mash the skinned bitter almonds to a pulp and add them to the chopped angelica stem. Mix these with the brandy and leave to soak for 5 days. Strain through nylon netting or muslin and stir in the sugar syrup. Bottle in small liqueur bottles, if these are available.

Salad Burnet
Sanguisorba minor

This hillside perennial is a lime-loving plant, but it is also especially fond of chalky districts. The stem is about 18 inches (45 cm) high, suberect or erect, branched and angular, often tinged with red, and the lower part sometimes downy. Its leaves are pinnate, having numerous small serrated leaflets on each side of a common stalk. From the end of June until the end of July we find it in flower, the upper part of the green round flowerhead bearing female florets with tufted crimson pistils, the lower ones (males) having pendulous red stamens with yellow anthers. There are some hermaphrodite (bearing both male and female organs) florets in the centre. It is void of petals; the calyx is square with four membranous sepals. The plant seems well able to flourish amid arid conditions.

If bruised the leaves smell of cucumber, and the plant owes its name of salad burnet to its leaves which our ancestors ate in salad, their taste being so like that of the cucumber. It seems that the plant makes excellent grazing for sheep, but that cattle are not particularly fond of it. In days gone by it was customary to infuse it in a variety of liquors, and two or three stalks if put in a cask of wine were said to 'quicken the spirits, refresh and clear the heart, and drive away melancholy'. It is nutritious and very astringent. The name burnet is derived from 'brunette' meaning 'brown', which is the colour of the flowers. *Sanguisorba* is Latin for 'blood-staunching' (*sanguis*, 'blood', and *sorbere*, 'to absorb').

Heather or Ling
Calluna vulgaris

Being a peat-loving plant, heaths and moorlands are essentially the homes of this evergreen, low-branched shrub which grows to heights of 1 to 2 feet (30 to 60 cm). The woody stems are reddish brown, wiry, and carry tiny branchlets; its tough fibrous perennial roots live from twenty to thirty years, throwing up fresh branches annually. The tiny, bright green leaves are arranged in four rows on opposite sides of the stem. They are stalkless, arrow-shaped, and overlap like roof tiles. They number thirty or so to every half inch (12 mm) which gives a good indication of the smallness in size. Their edges roll back, almost touching, to produce a tunnel into which all the water pores open; this helps minimize the amount of water given off by the plant, thereby helping it to withstand periods of drought. The flowers occur chiefly from July to September; they are small, bell-shaped and pinkish (occasionally white), horizontal or slightly drooping, and very numerous. The petals are much smaller than the sepals, indeed the pinkish sepals almost envelop them. The flowers remain on the plant long after the seeds have ripened. The seeds are in a capsule with many compartments and the capsules break off when dry, thus releasing the seeds.

A curious feature of the heather is its partnership with a root fungus. Together they live to each other's advantage: the fungus helps to absorb food from the peaty soil and passes it on, in a suitable form, to the plant; in return the fungus feeds upon the living sap of its host. This is a partnership known as symbiosis. *Calluna* is from the Greek *calluno* meaning 'I cleanse', alluding to the old custom of making brooms from its stems; because of this heather is sometimes referred to quite erroneously as broom; *vulgaris* refers to the plant's common occurrence.

Heather honey is regarded very highly and many say it is the most excellent of all the honies. A splendid tea can be made by infusing 3 tablespoons of fresh flowers (or

2 tablespoons of dried) in just under a pint (half a litre) of boiling water and leaving to stand for 5 minutes before straining.

A fine ale may be brewed from the plant as follows.

Heather beer

4 pints (2.5 l) heather flowers (on spikes)
8 pints (4.5 l) water
$\frac{1}{2}$ oz (15 g) ginger
2–3 cloves
$\frac{1}{4}$ oz (10 g) hops
$\frac{1}{2}$ lb (250 g) sugar
$\frac{1}{2}$ lb (250 g) malt
Yeast and nutrient

Add 7 pints (4 l) of the water to the flowers and bring to the boil; simmer for $1\frac{1}{2}$ hours. Strain and add the ginger and cloves; put on one side for the time being.

Place the hops in a smaller pan and add the remaining pint (600 ml) of water. Boil for 20 minutes and strain onto the sugar and malt. Bring back to the boil and simmer for 3 minutes. Allow to cool to room temperature before stirring in the yeast and nutrient (as for wine-making). Pour this into the pan containing the 'heather water', but check that the temperature of this liquid is not too high (needs to be about 35°C, 95°F or below). Cover and leave to ferment for 3 days. Skim off any deposit on the surface and syphon into beer bottles. Cap well and drink after about 3 weeks.

Bilberry or Whinberry
Vaccinium myrtillus

The bilberry is a typical heath plant, perhaps even more so of stony and mountainous places, but it may often be found on hillsides, in woods and copses on a soil rich in humus. It is also known as Huckleberry or Whortleberry. This shrubby plant seldom exceeds 18 inches (45 cm) in height. At first the stem is prostrate, later ascending and branched; it is smooth, green, angular, and rigid. The egg-shaped leaves are serrated and smooth, falling in the autumn. We find it in flower during the months of April, May and June. The flowers are solitary, greenish white tinged with red, wax-like and drooping. The fruit is an almost black or dark blue berry with a greyish bloom. Grouse and other moorland game birds are very fond of them. Goats and sheep will occasionally eat the leaves and shoots.

Vaccinium is the Latin name for the plant; *myrtillus* is from the Latin *myrtus*, 'myrtle', referring to the rich, deep myrtle-like greenness assumed by the leaves in autumn.

It has been known for these berries to be confused with those of deadly nightshade (*Atropa belladonna*), which is a fairly rare perennial that grows on sandy soil, chalk or limestone in waste places. It grows to heights of 2–4 ft (60–120 cm), the stem is herbaceous, stout, slightly hairy and branched, and the leaves are egg-shaped. The flowers are bell-shaped, dull purple, but streaked with yellow on the inside, and hang slightly. The berries are two-lobed, roundish, black and juicy. They are lethally poisonous (as is the entire plant) and should never be touched.

The fruit is ready for picking in the late summer and the best berries are found in sheltered situations. They may be eaten fresh or preserved by deep freezing or drying. In the Hebrides, the leaves were also dried and used as a substitute for tea.

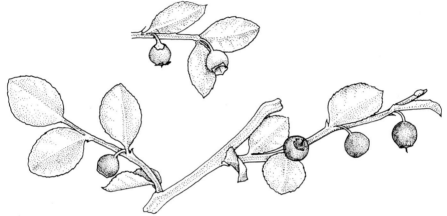

The juice from the fruit is used to produce purple dyes and herbalists recommend the berries be eaten to provide an astringent for those who suffer from diarrhoea.

Bilberries are juicy and tasty and can be used in any fruit recipe such as pies and crumbles. Bilberry jam is excellent and is often considered better than blackberry jam and not so seedy. A great deal of patience is needed, however, when collecting the required quantity of fruit.

Bilberry and Apple jelly

4 lb (2 kg) bilberries
2 lb (1 kg) cooking apples
Sugar
4 tablespoons water

Gently simmer the bilberries in 2 tablespoons of water until soft. Strain through a jelly-bag. Wipe and slice the apples and place in a pan. Add a little water and simmer gently to extract the apple juice. Strain through a jelly-bag overnight. Mix the two juices and measure the liquid, allowing 1 lb (500 g) of sugar for each pint (600 ml) of juice. Bring the juice to the boil and stir in the warmed sugar until dissolved. Boil rapidly until the jelly sets and then follow the standard procedure.

Bilberry wine

3 lb (1.5 kg) fresh bilberries
3 lb (1.5 kg) sugar
7 pints (4 l) water
½ tablespoon citric acid
Yeast and nutrient

Boil half the water and pour it over the bilberries. Add the sugar, stir to dissolve and when cool (about 30°C, 86°F), add the remaining cold water, the acid, yeast and nutrient. Cover well and leave for 3-4 days in a warm place. Strain through nylon netting or sieve into a fermenting jar and fit an air-lock. Rack for the first time when the wine clears and the wine should be ready for bottling after about six months.

Bilberry pudding

1 lb (500 g) bilberries
6 oz (150 g) sugar
1 small stale loaf of bread

Gently simmer the bilberries with the sugar until soft. Cut the bread into thick slices, remove the crusts and line the sides and bottom of a deep pudding basin with the bread, so that the slices overlap and there are no gaps. Keep a layer of bread aside for the top of the pudding. Place the bilberries and juice in the basin and cover the top with the remaining slice of bread. Place a saucer on the top with a heavy weight and leave in a fridge overnight. Serve chilled with cream or egg custard.

Bilberry pie

1 lb (500 g) bilberries
6 oz (150 g) sugar
1 teaspoon lemon juice
6 oz (150 g) shortcrust pastry

Roll out the pastry so that it is overlapping the top of the pie dish. Cut off the surplus and press it on the damp rim of the dish. Place the bilberries and sugar on the dish and sprinkle with lemon juice. Place a pie support in the centre and lay the pastry over it. Press the edges of the pastry together and place the pie on a baking tray in the centre of a hot oven (425°F, gas mark 6) for 15 minutes and then reduce to moderate heat (350°F, gas mark 4) for a further 15 minutes.

Bilberry jam

4 lb (2 kg) bilberries
1 lb (500 g) cooking apples
4 lb (2 kg) sugar
Juice of 1 lemon

It is important to use apple and lemon juice in the making of this jam, as bilberries have a low pectin content. Peel, core and slice the apples and place in a pan. Add a little water (1 tablespoon) and simmer gently to extract the apple juice. Strain through a jelly-bag. Place the bilberries in a pan with the lemon juice and simmer until soft. Remove from the heat, add the apple juice and warmed sugar and stir until all the sugar has dissolved. Boil rapidly until the jam sets when tested. Follow the standard procedure.

Bilberry soup

1 lb (500 g) bilberries
$\frac{3}{4}$ oz (20 g) cornflour
4 oz (100 g) sugar
Grated rind of $\frac{1}{2}$ lemon
1 pint (600 ml) water

Place the bilberries and lemon rind in the water and simmer until tender. Stir in the sugar and then remove from the heat. Blend the cornflour with a little water to form a smooth paste. Gradually stir into the soup, then bring to the boil, stirring continuously until the soup thickens.

Blackberry or Bramble
Rubus fruticosus

Bramble is a shrub excellently formed to serve as a hedge plant; its long stems intertwine quickly and readily with the branches of other hedgerow plants. The stems are furnished with numerous large backward-pointing barbs which in no way hinder the plant's growth as it pushes between other hedge plants; but as anyone who has attempted to extricate a bramble stem will know these sharp hooks make the task very difficult.

Brambles exhibit great variability, with many different kinds being recognized, but in general the leaf has a smooth face, the underside a coating of hairs and a series of small prickles running up the midrib. In autumn the tints are in shades of red and russet. Flowering usually extends from June to October; each bloom consists of five finely pointed sepals and these turn downwards as the blossom begins to mature. The petals are five in number and may be pure white or tinged with pink; the stamens

are numerous and crowded together to form a thick ring in the centre of which, and raised above all else, are the many carpels. The blackberry has what the botanists call an 'aggregate fruit', with each small and separate ovary developing to become a black fleshy globule and containing a seed; twenty or more of these may combine to form the 'blackberry'. As a matter of interest let us compare a blackberry with a strawberry. The hard yellow specks on the outside of the latter are equivalent to the juicy black globules of the blackberry; with the dry stalk-end of the blackberry being the equivalent of the strawberry's red flesh.

In ancient times both flowers and fruit were regarded as a cure for a serpent's bite. Roman physicians would boil the roots in wine and administer as an astringent. A decoction of the fruit is still recognized as effective for soreness both of the mouth and the throat. It is said that the silkworm will feed on its leaves and spin cocoons of high quality silk. In the past a black dye was prepared from the stem.

Do not confuse with the berries of deadly nightshade (*see* p. 83).

Blackberries are good any way they are eaten and are a useful source of Vitamin C. A generation ago, blackberry-picking was a major event for both town and country people and the hedgerows were raided by entire families. Few households were without blackberry jam or jelly during the cold winter months. Some people used them for dyeing, and the colour navy blue was originally produced with blackberry juice. During times of severe hardship, blackberries have replaced currants in buns, and have even been used to sweeten cooked parsnips and beetroot.

Although it is the best known wild fruiting plant, there have been cases of confusion with other inedible black fruit. This is surprising, since the only other wild fruit which resembles the blackberry is the equally delicious dewberry which belongs to the same family.

The first berry to ripen is the lowest one, found right at the tip of the stalk. It is usually the juiciest and sweetest of all. A good way of serving the berries at this stage is to soak them overnight in red wine and then serve with cream the following day. The smaller berries further up the stalk tend to ripen much later and are rather 'seedy'. They should then be cooked with other fruit for best results.

Blackberry cordial

2 pints (1200 ml) ripe blackberries
1 pint (600 ml) white vinegar
$\frac{1}{2}$ lb (250 g) honey
1 lb (500 g) sugar

Mix the vinegar with the blackberries in an earthenware jar and allow to stand for a week, stirring daily. Strain the mixture through a jelly-bag overnight. Mix the liquid with the sugar and honey and bring to the boil. Allow to cool and pour the cordial into clean, dry bottles. Cork and store in a dark place.

This syrup can be diluted with water for a refreshing drink, and is excellent for colds and sore throats.

Blackberry jelly

2 lb (1 kg) blackberries
$\frac{1}{4}$ pint (150 ml) water
Juice of 2 lemons
Sugar

Simmer the blackberries, lemon juice and water in the pan until soft; strain overnight through a jelly-bag. Measure the juice and for each pint allow 1 lb (500 g) of sugar. Bring the juice to the boil, add the warmed sugar and stir until dissolved. Boil rapidly until the mixture sets when tested. Follow the standard procedure for jelly-making as set out in the Introduction.

Spiced Blackberry jelly

Follow the above recipe but add half a teaspoonful each of mace, nutmeg and cinnamon to the blackberries, water and lemon juice, when simmering.

Blackberry and Crab Apple jelly

2 lb (1 kg) blackberries
1 lb (500 g) crab apples
½ pint (300 ml) water
Sugar
Juice of 1 lemon

The juice from the two fruits should be obtained separately. Simmer the black-berries, lemon juice and ¼ pint of water until soft, then strain through a jelly-bag. Cut the apples in half and simmer with the remaining ¼ pint of water until soft; allow to strain through a jelly-bag overnight.

The two juices can now be mixed together and measured. Allow 1 lb (500 g) of sugar for each pint of juice. Bring the juice to the boil and stir in the warmed sugar until dissolved. Boil rapidly until the jelly sets, and then follow the standard procedure as set out in the Introduction.

Blackberry and Elderberry jam

2 lb (1 kg) blackberries
2 lb (1 kg) elderberries
1 lb (500 g) apples
4 lb (2 kg) sugar
Juice of 1 lemon
¾ pint (450 ml) water

Peel, core and slice the apples and place in a pan with ½ pint of water. Boil the apples to a pulp and strain through a jelly-bag. Place the blackberries, elderberries, lemon juice and the remaining water in the pan. Bring to the boil and simmer until soft. Add the apple juice and warmed sugar and stir until all the sugar has dissolved. Boil rapidly until the mixture sets when tested. Follow the standard procedure for jam-making as set out in the Introduction.

Blackberry wine

4 lb (2 kg) blackberries
3 lb (1.5 kg) sugar
7 pints (4 l) water
Pectic enzyme
Yeast and nutrient

Pick whole, clean berries and wash them well. Crush with a wooden spoon and pour boiling water over them. Stir well and allow to cool. When it is at room temperature, add the recommended quantity of pectic enzyme. Cover, and a day later stir in the yeast and nutrient, then leave covered for a further four days, stirring daily. Strain through nylon netting, or sieve, and add the sugar, stirring well to dissolve it all. Pour into dark fermenting jars up to the shoulder, and fit an air-lock. When the fermentation has quietened down after a week or so, top up to the bottom of the neck with cold water and re-fit the air-lock. Allow to clear before racking for the first time; this is usually after 2–3 months.

Blackberry and Rowanberry jelly

2 lb (1 kg) blackberries
3 lb (1.5 kg) rowanberries
$\frac{3}{4}$ pint (450 ml) water
Sugar

This is a sharp-tasting jelly. Place the rowanberries in a pan with a $\frac{1}{4}$ pint (150 ml) of water and boil for approximately 30 minutes, stirring occasionally, and then strain through a jelly-bag. Next, place the blackberries and the remaining water in a different pan and simmer for 20 minutes or until the fruit is soft. Strain through a jelly-bag. Measure the two juices and place equal quantities of each in the pan and allow 1 pound (500 g) of sugar for each pint (600 ml) of juice. Bring the liquid to the boil, add the warmed sugar and stir until dissolved. Continue to boil the mixture and start testing for setting after 25 minutes. Follow the jelly-making procedure as set out in the Introduction.

Blackberry fool

8 oz (250 g) blackberries
1 tablespoon sugar
2 teaspoons vanilla essence
Whipped cream
Water

Place the blackberries in a pan and just cover with water. Simmer until the berries are soft. Add the sugar and vanilla essence and stir until dissolved. Rub the mixture through a sieve. Fold the cream into the blackberries and serve chilled.

Blackberry and Sloe jelly

8 lb (4 kg) blackberries
2 lb (1 kg) sloes
$2\frac{1}{2}$ pints (1.5 l) water
5 lb (2.5 kg) sugar

Place the blackberries, sloes and water in a pan and bring to the boil. Continue boiling until the fruit appears to look as if it has been bleached and then strain through a jelly-bag overnight. About 7 pints of liquid should be obtained. Bring it again to the boil and add 5 pounds (2.5 kg) of warmed sugar, stirring until dissolved. Boil rapidly and test for setting after 20 minutes. Follow the standard procedure for jelly-making as set out in the Introduction.

Blackberry jam

6 lb (3 kg) blackberries
2 lb (1 kg) apples
6 lb (3 kg) sugar
Juice of 1 lemon
1 pint (600 ml) water

Peel, core and slice the apples and place in a pan with $\frac{3}{4}$ pint (450 ml) of water. Boil the apples to a pulp and strain through a jelly-bag. Place the blackberries, lemon juice and remaining water in a pan and simmer until soft. Add the apple juice and warmed sugar and stir until dissolved. Boil rapidly until the jam sets when tested. Follow the standard procedure for jam-making as set out in the Introduction.

Blackberry and Crab Apple jam

4 lb (2 kg) blackberries
4 lb (2 kg) crab apples
8 lb (4 kg) sugar
Rind of 2 lemons
$1\frac{1}{2}$ pints (900 ml) water

Peel, core and slice the crab apples and place in a pan with 1 pint (600 ml) of water. Boil the apples to a pulp and add the grated lemon rind. Simmer the blackberries in the remaining $\frac{1}{2}$ pint of water until soft, then mix with the apples. Add the warmed sugar and stir until dissolved. Boil rapidly until the jam sets when tested. Follow the standard procedure on jam-making as set out in the Introduction.

Blackberry pie

1 lb (500 g) blackberries
6 oz (150 g) shortcrust pastry
3 oz (75 g) sugar
2 tablespoons water

Roll out the pastry so that it is overlapping the top of the pie dish. Cut the surplus off and press it on the damp rim of the dish. Place the blackberries, sugar and water in a pan and simmer for approximately 5 minutes. Pour the mixture into the pie dish, position a pie support in the centre, and lay the pastry over. Press the edges of both layers of pastry together and place the pie on a baking tray in the centre of a hot oven (420°F, gas mark 6) for 15-20 minutes, then reduce to moderate heat (350°, gas mark 4) for a further 15 minutes.

Blackberry and Elderberry chutney

2 lb (1 kg) blackberries
2 lb (1 kg) elderberries
3 lb (1.5 kg) cooking apples
1 lb (500 g) onions
½ lb (250 g) raisins
2 pints (1200 ml) malt vinegar
8 oz (250 g) brown sugar
2 teaspoons salt
2 teaspoons pickling spices
2 teaspoons ground ginger
1 teaspoon mustard

Wash the blackberries and elderberries. Peel, core and chop the apples and place with the blackberries and elderberries in a pan. Pour on the vinegar and mash well. Chop the onions and raisins, and add together with the remaining ingredients to the mashed fruit. Simmer the mixture for approximately 15 minutes, stirring all the time. When it thickens, pour into warm jars and seal well.

Cranberry or Marsh Whortleberry
Vaccinium oxycoccus

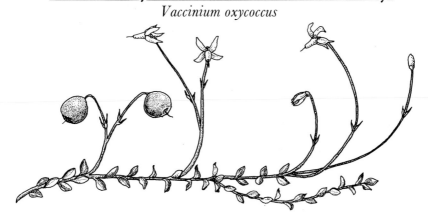

The cranberry is a very local plant growing in spongy peat-bogs in company with *Sphagnum* (and other bog-mosses), Sundew, Butterwort, Bog Asphodel etc, and usually at elevation. This low, straggling, perennial bush grows in patches, and it has tough wiry branches of 8 to 10 inches (20 to 25 cm) long, with stems no more than 3 inches (8 cm) high. The tiny leaves are egg-shaped, glaucous on the underside, have a turned-back margin, and are evergreen. Its flowers are in bloom from June to August, each one lasting for a period of almost three weeks. They are borne singly at the end of long slender stalks, bright red in colour, and with the segments of the corolla turned back. The berry is red and edible with a pleasant acid flavour, and much sought after for culinary purposes (although this does not, or did not, apply in Sweden where they are plentiful but used solely for cleaning silver or other metal kitchen utensils).

The English name of cranberry is thought to have been derived from the flower-stalks which, before the blossom expands, is crooked at the top and said to resemble the arched neck and head of the crane; or simply because it is ripe when the cranes appear (probably many years ago in Britain the grey heron was referred to as a crane). The specific name *oxycoccus* is from the Greek *oxys*, meaning 'sharp'; and *coccus*, a 'fruit' or 'berry', alluding to the cranberry's sharp or acid flavour. They are a good astringent, and would most likely help revive a poor appetite.

Cranberry chutney

4 pints (2.5 l) cranberries
$3\frac{1}{2}$ lb (1.75 kg) sugar
8 oz (250 g) chopped onion
1 lb (500 g) chopped raisins
$\frac{1}{2}$ pint (300 ml) vinegar
Chopped rind of 2 oranges
Juice of 2 oranges
1 teaspoon each ground ginger, cinnamon, powdered cloves, salt and pepper
$\frac{1}{2}$ oz (15 g) mustard seed

Place all the ingredients in a pan and boil until the mixture thickens. Pour into sterilized bottles and seal.

Cranberry sauce

1 lb (500 g) cranberries
4 oz (100 g) sugar
2 glasses port wine
1 teacup water

Place the cranberries and water in a pan; simmer until the fruit is soft and then press through a sieve. Add the sugar, reheat and before serving add the port wine. This sauce is traditionally served at Christmas with turkey.

Cranberry and Apple jelly

1½ lb (750 g) cranberries
1½ lb (750 g) cooking apples
3 lb (1.5 kg) sugar
½ pint (300 ml) water

Peel, core and slice the apples; wash the cranberries and place all the fruit in a pan with the water. Simmer until the fruit is soft, but not mushy (approximately 15 minutes). Add the warmed sugar and stir until dissolved. Boil rapidly until the jam sets when tested (approximately 10 minutes). Follow the usual procedure.

Cranberry relish

8 oz (250 g) cranberries
1 apple
1 orange
1 lemon
8 oz (250 g) sugar

Wash the cranberries; core the apple, but do not peel, and blend together in an electric blender. Remove the pips from the orange and lemon, and mince them finely. Add to the cranberry mixture together with the sugar and mix well. Pour into jars and cover. It should be eaten fairly soon as it does not keep very well.

Cranberry and Apple jam

2 lb (1 kg) cranberries
3 lb (1.5 kg) cooking apples
Water
Sugar

Wash the fruit and slice the apples; place in a pan with enough water to cover. Simmer slowly until soft and mushy, then strain through a jelly-bag overnight. Measure the juice and for each pint allow 1 pound (500 g) of sugar. Bring the juice to the boil, add the warmed sugar and stir until dissolved. Boil rapidly until the jelly sets when tested. Remove the scum and follow the normal procedure on jelly-making.

Cranberry cheese

1½ lb (750 g) cranberries
1½ lb (750 g) sugar
1½ pints (900 ml) water

Wash the cranberries and place in a pan with the water. Simmer until the fruit is soft; then rub through a sieve with a wooden spoon. Wash out the pan before return-ing the cranberry purée to it. Stir in the sugar until dissolved and then bring to the boil, stirring continuously. When a semi-solid consistency is achieved, the cheese is ready for potting. Follow the same procedure as for jam-making. Cranberry cheese is excellent served with roast turkey or game.

Dewberry
Rubus caesius

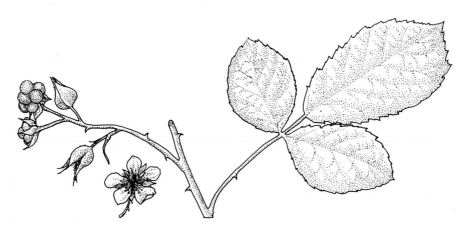

The dewberry is a low-growing bramble whose stems are rooting, and prostrate or arched with a trailing habit. It is usually found in damp places and is not uncommon in thickets, hedges, field borders or heaths. It is often found on a sandy substrate. The stem is round and bluish-white, and the awl-like prickles are weak, short, scattered and unequal. The leaves are ternate or quinate (3 or 5 leaflets on a leaf-stalk), the underside is not covered in a white down. Flowering continues from June to late August, a few white flowers in a loose panicle. The fruits are large and few, less compact than the blackberry but more juicy, with the long pointed sepals partially enclosing the drupelets. They are black when ripe but quite often thickly covered in a pale blue pubescence as to give them a greyish cast, occurring singly or perhaps two or three together, and not densely clustered as in the blackberry.

Dewberries ripen before blackberries, and although they do not have quite as good a flavour they can be used in the same ways.

Elderberries

(For a description of the plant see pp. 72-3.)

The elderberry is rich in vitamins A, B and C and in the elements potassium, iron and calcium; its medicinal properties have long since been noted. A cordial made from boiling the berries with a few drops of peppermint and a little honey helps to alleviate troublesome colds and coughs.

The best time to pick the berries is when they have just turned black and the clusters have turned upside down. The clusters should be cut from the stems and washed, and the berries removed from the stalks by a fork. The berries, added to stewed apples or gooseberries, greatly improve their flavour.

Elderberry jelly

4 lb (2 kg) elderberries
6 tablespoons lemon juice
Sugar
1 pint (600 ml) water

Simmer the fruit, lemon juice and water for approximately 50 minutes. Strain through a jelly-bag overnight. Measure the liquid and allow ¾ lb (350 g) sugar for each pint (600 ml) of juice. Bring the mixture to the boil, add the warmed sugar and stir until dissolved. Boil until the jelly sets and proceed as stated in the section on jelly-making in the Introduction.

Elderberry and Crab Apple jelly

4 pints (2.5 l) elderberries (after picking from stalks)
3 lb (1.5 kg) crab apples
2 pints (1200 ml) water
Sugar

Wash the apples and cut into pieces, removing any bruised parts: there is no need to peel and core. Place the apples with the elderberries and water in a pan and simmer to a pulp. Strain the mixture through a jelly-bag overnight. Measure the juice and allow one pound (500 g) of sugar for each pint of juice. Bring the juice to the boil, add the warmed sugar and stir until dissolved. Boil rapidly until the jelly sets when tested, then follow the standard procedure set out in the Introduction.

Elderberry pickle

1 lb (500 g) elderberries
1 small onion
2 tablespoons sugar
$\frac{1}{2}$ pint (300 ml) vinegar
$\frac{1}{2}$ teaspoon ground ginger
$\frac{1}{4}$ teaspoon mixed spice
Pinch of salt

Place the elderberries in a pan and mash them well. Chop the onion and add with all the other ingredients to the berries. Bring to the boil and simmer slowly until the mixture thickens. Stir continuously to stop the mixture sticking to the pan. Pour immediately into hot sterilized jars and seal.

Elderberry syrup

5 lb (2.5 kg) elderberries
$1\frac{1}{2}$ pints (900 ml) water
Sugar

Place the elderberries with the water in a pan, bring to the boil and simmer for 40 minutes. Strain overnight through a jelly-bag. Measure the juice and allow 6 ounces (200 g) of sugar for each pint (600 ml). Bring the juice back to the boil and simmer for 10 minutes. Add the warmed sugar and stir until it is dissolved. Again bring the liquid back to the boil and simmer for a further 20 minutes. Skim off the scum and pour into sterilized bottles and cap securely.

Elderberry wine

3 lb (1.5 kg) elderberries
3 lb (1.5 kg) sugar
7 pints (4 l) water
Yeast and nutrient

Crush the berries with a wooden spoon and pour the boiling water onto them. Allow to cool to room temperature before stirring in the yeast and nutrient. Cover and leave for 3 days, stirring daily. Strain through a fine nylon sieve and stir in the sugar until all has dissolved. Pour into a dark fermenting jar, up to the shoulder, and fit an air-lock. When the initial fermentation has subsided, top up to the neck with cold water and re-fit the lock. Rack for the first time when the fermentation is complete; this may be up to 6 months. After bottling, keep for 9–12 months before drinking.

Elderberry soup

1½ lb (750 g) elderberries
¾ oz (20 g) cornflour
4 oz (100 g) sugar
Grated rind of ½ lemon
2 pints (1200 ml) water

Place the elderberries and lemon rind in the water and simmer until tender. Stir in the sugar and remove from the heat. Blend the cornflour with a little water to form a smooth paste. Gradually add this to the soup, then bring back to the boil stirring continuously until it thickens.

Elderberry sauce

1 pint (600 ml) elderberries
1 pint (600 ml) claret
1 finely chopped onion
1 teaspoon salt
4 peppercorns
1 stick bruised root ginger

Bring the claret to the boil and pour over the elderberries in a casserole dish. Cover and place in a low heated oven overnight. Strain the juice into a pan, add the remaining ingredients and boil for 10 minutes. Pour the sauce into sterilized bottles and seal. This sauce makes a fine accompaniment with liver.

Elderberry vinegar

12 oz (350 g) elderberries
1 pint (600 ml) white vinegar
12 oz (350 g) sugar

Wash the elderberries, place in jars with the vinegar and leave to stand for 6 days, shaking occasionally. Strain through a jelly-bag and place the liquid in a pan with the sugar. Stir until the sugar has dissolved, then bring to the boil. Bottle the vinegar when it has cooled, seal and store in a dry place. Elderberry vinegar can be drunk hot to relieve sore throats, or cold as a reviving drink on a summer's day.

Sea Lettuce
Ulva lactuca

Tansy
Chrysanthemum vulgare

Cranberries
Vaccinium oxycoccos

Salad Burnet
Sanguisorba minor

Bilberries *(Vaccinium myrtillus)*
in heather *(Calluna vulgaris)*

Fennel
Foeniculum vulgare

Sessile Oak
Quercus petraea

Wild Angelica
Angelica sylvestris

Beech nuts
Fagus sylvatica

Dewberry
Rubus caesius

Elderberries
Sambucus nigra

Blackberry
Rubus fruticosus

Haws
Crataegus monogyna

Cep
Boletus edulis

Field Mushroom
Agaricus campestris

Horse Mushroom
Agaricus arvensis

Giant Puff-ball
Langermannia gigantea

Chanterelle
Cantharellus cibarius

Hawthorn berries
(For a description of the plant see pp. 33–4.)

Hawthorn berry jelly

3 lb (1.5 kg) haws
2 pints (1200 ml) water
Juice of 3 lemons
Sugar

Pick the berries when they are ripe and juicy. Wash them well and place in a preserving pan with the water. Simmer for 60 minutes, mashing the fruit every 15 minutes. Strain through a jelly-bag overnight. Measure the liquid and allow 1 pound (500 g) of sugar for each pint. Reheat the liquid and add the warmed sugar and lemon juice and stir over a low heat until the sugar has dissolved. Boil rapidly until the jelly sets when tested. Follow the standard procedure. Hawthorn jelly is excellent served with cold meat.

Hawthorn and Crab Apple jelly

1 lb (500 g) haws
2 lb (1 kg) crab apples
1 pint (600 ml) water
Juice of 1 lemon
Sugar

Wash and dry the fruit. Slice the apples (there is no need to peel and core) and place them with the haws and water in the preserving pan. Simmer for 60 minutes, mashing the fruit frequently. Strain through a jelly-bag overnight. Measure the liquid and for each pint (600 ml) of juice allow 1 pound (500 g) of sugar. Reheat the liquid and stir in the warmed sugar and lemon juice over a low heat, ensuring that the sugar dissolves completely. Then boil rapidly until the jelly sets when tested. Follow the standard procedure.

Beech
Fagus sylvatica

The beech is a deciduous tree that grows, as a rule, to heights of between 40 and 60 feet (12 and 18 metres), and under exceptional circumstances to twice that height. It can be found either as a tree with two main branches and very lofty; or with horizontal spreading branches at a much lower level. The beech likes a lime soil rich in humus and well drained, which need not necessarily be deep. Inside the buds its leaves are folded like a fan. They begin to open in spring and the tree is in full leaf

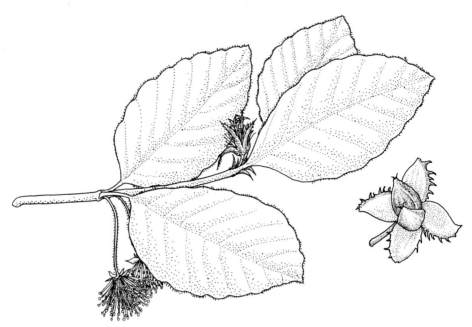

by the end of May. They are egg-shaped, pointed and smooth, with a slightly wavy, finely toothed margin that is delicately fringed with fine silvery hairs. At first the leaves are emerald green and almost translucid; gradually they darken, become thicker, and lose the fringe of hairs.

The beech tree seems not to flower every year or to produce far fewer in some years than others; but when it does then both male and female flowers occur on the same tree (monoecious). They appear during April and May, shortly after or at the same time as the leaves. The males hang catkin-like, purplish brown flower heads with yellow anthers, at the end of 1 to 2 inch (25 to 50 mm) stalks. The females are produced in clusters of 2 or 3, they are enclosed in a cupula of overlapping scales, and have their styles projecting from the top. After shedding their pollen the male flowers soon fall away, leaving the fertile females to develop into those familiar rounded and bristly boxes which split open at one end, then fold backwards in four quarters to reveal and later release the two or more, small, brown, 3-sided, sharp edged nuts or 'beech-mast'.

Fagus is the Latin name for beech, and *sylvatica* is indicative of its woodland habitat. The common name of beech is derived from the Anglo-Saxon *boc*, *bece*, or *beoce*. Ancient Scandinavian and German literature is said to have been inscribed on tablets of Beech, and so the word 'book' is from the same origin. Other common names include Buck-mast and Hay Beech. The thin beech bark was once used in basket work.

The nuts, although small when peeled, provide a valuable source of protein and contain trace elements such as magnesium, calcium, phosphorus and potassium. In the past, they have been eaten by poorer families and their merit as a food source was recognized in Germany during the war when schoolchildren were given extra holidays to collect them.

The nut when eaten raw has a slightly bitter taste, but this disappears when roasted. Roasted beech nuts can be eaten with salads or ground and used as a sub-stitute for coffee. Oil can be extracted from the nuts in the following manner: first roast the nuts in a hot oven, then mince them to a pulp through a mincer or liquidizer. Place the pulp in a muslin bag and extract the oil by pressing down with a heavy weight. It should be stored in sterilized jars and tightly covered; it keeps better than most vegetable oils and can be used for frying and other cooking. It also makes an excellent salad dressing.

Beech leaf liqueur

1 pint (600 ml) young beech leaves (pressed down lightly)
$\frac{3}{4}$ pint (450 ml) gin
$\frac{1}{2}$ lb (250 g) honey

Cram the beech leaves into a deep glass jar and pour the gin over them, making sure the leaves are completely covered. Cover well and leave for a fortnight before strain-ing. Dissolve the honey in as little hot water as necessary and mix thoroughly into the gin. Bottle when the liqueur has cooled.

Pedunculate Oak and Sessile Oak
Quercus robur   *Quercus petraea*

Both species are indigenous to Britain. The pedunculate oak shows a preference for the lower hills and valley sides of the eastern and southern counties, whereas the sessile oak is the dominant species in Scotland, north and west England and Wales, preferring higher ground but with a western or southern aspect. Oak trees usually range in height from 50 to 100 feet (15 to 30 metres), and show a considerable degree of variation which may be due to differences in soil or differences in situation. The trunk is thick and usually short, with several long and massive branches; many of the lower ones are horizontal, the upper ones ascending or spreading (never droop-ing) usually forming an angle or elbow, and so presenting a twisted appearance. The trunk of the sessile oak is often longer, less stout, and the branches straighter than the pedunculate oak, but the two hybridize freely making positive identification difficult at times.

During late April and May the leaves begin to unfurl. At first they are pale green, later becoming much darker. Those of the pedunculate oak have 4 to 5 quite deep lobes on each side and a very short leaf-stalk $\frac{1}{5}$ t $\frac{2}{5}$ of an inch (5 to 10 mm) long, whereas the sessile oak usually has from 5 to 8 shallow lobes on each side of the leaf and the stalk $\frac{1}{2}$ to 1 inch (12 to 25 mm) long. The flowers appear with the leaves and both sexes are borne on the same tree; the slender male catkins are composed of small greenish yellow flower clusters, borne at intervals along a 2 to 3 inch (50 to

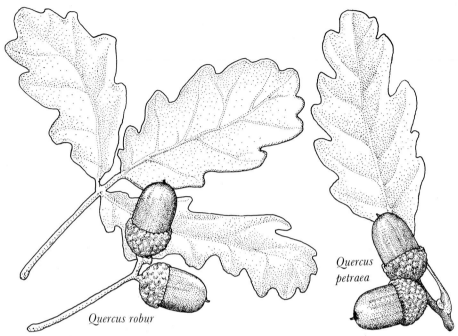

Quercus petraea

Quercus robur

75 mm) hanging stalk. The round, brown female flowers are far fewer and consist of a calyx clothed in a number of small overlapping scales (which will later develop to become a shallow cup holding the nut). Inside there is an ovary with three styles. These are borne singly or in small groups on short (sessile oak) or long (pedunculate oak) stiff stalks above the male catkins and emanate from leaf axils at the end of a shoot.

Perhaps the two oaks are most easily identified from their fruit, the acorn; in the pedunculate these are borne on stalks of $1\frac{1}{2}$ to 3 inches (4 to 8 cm) in length, and in the sessile the acorns are without stalks or on very short ones. Each acorn is a single-seeded, almost egg-shaped, nut resting in a shallow cup of close overlapping scales. The fruit ripens and falls to the ground in October; seldom does the oak produce a heavy crop of acorns until it is over 60 years old. Oakwood is hard, strong, straight-grained and durable; it is suitable for work both indoors and out. The uses include flooring, doors, roof beams, furniture, and boat-building. The name oak comes from the Anglo-Saxon *āc*.

In times of famine and hardship, acorns were often boiled and ground into flour, and then made into bread. When chopped and roasted they can be used instead of almonds and also as a coffee substitute as was the case during the Second World War. To prepare the coffee, chop the nuts roughly and place in a moderately hot oven to roast. Allow them to cool, grind and then return to the oven until they are well roasted. Pour boiling water over the roasted ground nuts, stir and leave to steep for 10 minutes. The coffee is ready to drink after straining and is said to be very soothing.

Oakleaf wine

7 pints (4 l) oak leaves
3 lb (1.5 kg) sugar
7 pints (4 l) water
Juice of 2 lemons
Yeast and nutrient

Wash the leaves in cold water and allow the water to drain off. Bring 5 pints (3 l) of water to the boil and dissolve the sugar in it. Pour the boiling liquid over the leaves, cover and allow to stand overnight. The following day, strain into a fermenting jar and add the lemon juice, yeast and nutrient. Fill up with the remaining water to the bottom of the neck. Shake the jar thoroughly and fit an air-lock. Rack for the first time when the wine clears and then a few months later. Bottle after about 6 months.

Walnut leaves may be used as an alternative to oak leaves, should they be available.

Cep or Edible Boletus
Boletus edulis

From August to November the edible boletus is a fairly common species which can be found on the ground in both coniferous and frondose woodlands, but predominantly in the latter, and especially beech. It grows singly or in small scattered groups, and the margins of woodlands are also well worth attention. It is usually about 6 inches (15 cm) tall and with a cap diameter of similar dimension; however, larger specimens do occur. The cap colour may vary considerably but is usually some shade of brown and darker at the centre, dry, smooth, and shining or slightly viscid, sometimes with a wrinkled surface. The small round pores on the underside of the cap are at first off-white, later yellowish, and finally greenish-yellow; they do not bruise purple. The spores are usually olive-brown. The stem is robust and solid, typically pestle-shaped, or irregularly swollen from middle to base. It is whitish or pale brownish shading lighter basally and has a raised network of fine white veins on the surface of the upper stem. This closely meshed network sometimes covers the entire stem surface. The flesh is mainly white, sometimes with a suggestion of pink, and it does not change colour when broken or bruised. It is firm in young specimens, becoming softer with age. The edible boletus has a pleasant odour and a mild nutty flavour. It is rated as one of the best edible species, and is highly esteemed in Europe where it is widely marketed. Other common names include Penny-bun Bolete, and in North America King Boletus.

Many other boleti are edible but those which are reddish or pinkish on the stem or under the cap should be avoided as they are bitter and unpalatable, although not poisonous. Fresh ceps contain vitamin D. When gathering, check carefully for maggots by cutting the specimens in half. To prepare for eating, discard the tubes and if the stem is sound cut it into slices for cooking with the cap.

They can be used in all the same ways as mushrooms. If used raw in salads, small quantities only should be eaten. They are excellent as a vegetable, fried, stewed or baked; some prefer them deep-fried with a coating of egg and breadcrumbs. Ceps make a delicious sauce and can also be stuffed or used in a stuffing. They are particularly suitable for drying and in this form are used in flavouring soups, casseroles, stews and gravies.

Ceps with scrambled eggs

Ceps or other edible boleti
1 onion
Parsley
Salt and pepper
1 oz (25 g) butter
Scrambled egg—allow 1 egg and 1 tablespoon milk per person

Chop the onion finely and fry in the melted butter. Add the sliced boleti discarding the tubes and continue to fry for 15 minutes, when all the water should have evaporated. Prepare the eggs by beating well and mixing with the milk. Pour into the frying pan and add the chopped parsley, salt and pepper. Serve hot with toast. Chanterelles can be used in place of ceps.

Fried Ceps

Large ceps
1 egg
Flour
Breadcrumbs
Salt
1 oz (25 g) butter

Thickly slice the ceps and sprinkle with salt and flour. Turn over the ceps in the beaten egg and then coat well with the breadcrumbs. Melt the butter and fry the coated fungi slices until they are golden brown on both sides.

Stewed Ceps

2 lb (1 kg) ceps
3 onions
1 tablespoon flour
3 oz (75 g) butter
Salt and pepper
Chopped parsley

Melt the butter in a pan and add the quartered ceps and the whole onions. Cover and cook for 20 minutes. Remove the onions and sprinkle the ceps with the flour. Add some hot vegetable stock if the mixture becomes too tacky. Season with salt and pepper and sprinkle with chopped parsley. Serve with rice or potatoes.

Chanterelle
Cantharellus cibarius

The chanterelle may be looked for on the ground in all types of woodland; often amongst beds of moss. It is locally common, the season extending from June to November. It is typically deep golden yellow, but variable. Some specimens are a very pale yellow, and it has a tendency to pale with age. When it first pushes through the soil it is small, stubby and top-shaped; it eventually grows up to 3 inches (7.5 cm) tall and becomes funnel-shaped with a central depression. The cap is up to 4 inches (10 cm) across, smooth and unevenly lobed, incurved, and irregularly wavy. The gills are vein-like, broad but shallow, narrow-folded, and decurrent (extending downward onto upper part of stem). It has a shortish, stout, solid stem which is continuous with the cap, and narrows downwards, often curved at the base. As it dries, it emits a pleasant aroma of apricots, but this is not perceptible to everyone. Both gills and stem are more or less concolorous with the cap. It should not be confused with the false chanterelle (*Hygrophoropsis aurantiaca*), which is very common in coniferous woodlands and heathland from late summer to autumn. Its deep orange or orange-red gills are true, and not folded as in *C. cibarius*; it has neither an apricot-like aroma nor a pleasant taste, but it is harmless. The spores are white, not pinkish-buff as in the true chanterelle.

The chanterelle contains vitamins A and D. Due to its colour and shape, it is easy to find and identify and is rarely attacked by insects. It is one of the most popular edible fungi on the Continent where it is regarded as a delicacy.

For eating collect only the young specimens which are not over-ripe and rotting. Do not roast them, but cook slowly in a little milk until tender so that none of their excellent flavour is lost. Their spicy taste gives an added tang to egg and vegetable dishes. They are excellent fried with scrambled eggs or cooked and served in omelettes. They can also be used in salads, stews, soups, sauces and stuffings.

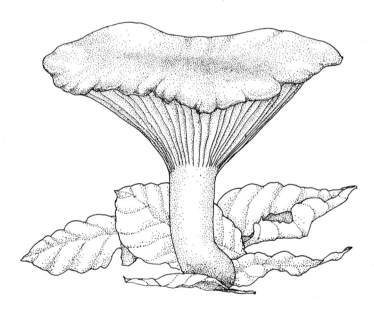

Chanterelle omelette

1½ lb (750 g) chanterelles
4 eggs
1 tablespoon chopped onion
1 tablespoon chopped parsley
2½ oz (65 g) margarine
Salt and pepper

Melt 1 oz (25 g) of the margarine in a pan and fry the onions. Cut the chanterelles into quarters, add with the chopped parsley to the onion, and continue frying until tender. Whisk the eggs and seasoning. Heat the remaining margarine in a frying pan and pour in the eggs. Continue as if preparing an ordinary omelette, and when all the liquid is lightly set place the chanterelle mixture on top. Fold in half and serve piping hot.

Chanterelles and tomatoes

1 lb (500 g) chanterelles
5 large tomatoes
1 onion finely chopped
3 tablespoons top of the milk
1 tablespoon lemon juice
1 oz (25 g) margarine
Salt and pepper
Flour
Chopped parsley

Melt the margarine and fry the onion. Quarter the chanterelles, slice the tomatoes and add to the onion. Season well and cook for 10 minutes. Sprinkle the mixture with flour, add the top of the milk and lemon juice and simmer gently until the chanterelles are tender. Sprinkle with chopped parsley before serving.

Giant Puff-ball
Langermannia gigantea (Lycoperdon gigantea)

The giant puff-ball grows in meadows and pastures, as well as on golf courses, lawns,

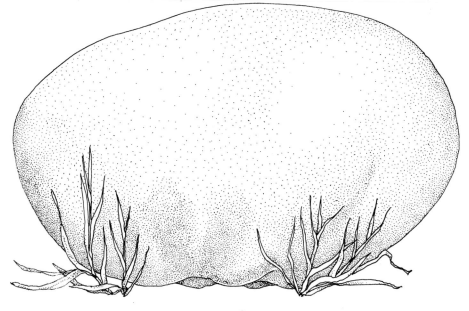

grassy roadside verges, sometimes grassy clearings in woodlands, and decomposed vegetable matter such as old compost heaps. It is often found in the same spot in successive years. It is locally common, occurring during late summer or early autumn (occasionally spring), usually gregarious but sometimes growing singly. The enormous size is a sufficient guide to identification. The diameter varies from 2 to 20 inches (5 to 50 cm), and is sometimes even larger. It is creamy-white and globose with a slight depression, smooth and with the texture of chamois leather; it is somewhat corrugated towards the base, and attached to the substrate by thick strands of mycelium. The flesh or gleba is white and firm at first, later yellowish and finally olive brown and powdery. As it matures so the spherical shape changes to oval. Eventually the outer skin splits to reveal the thin brittle inner skin, which subsequently cracks and collapses thus permitting the liberation of several thousand million brown spores. Its common French name *Tête de Mort* is given because of its resemblance to the bleached skull of a human.

A large specimen found during the war was thought to be a new type of German bomb. In past times the fungi was collected and dried for tinder and it has also been used by countryfolk to staunch bleeding.

The giant puff-ball is only edible when young, whilst the flesh is white and firm. It is excellent when thickly sliced and fried in bacon fat until golden brown; it can also be mixed with other edible fungi for cooking.

Field Mushroom
Agaricus campestris

This is a common edible species much sought after in fields, meadows and other grassy places, from July to November. It occurs singly or in scattered groups and grows up to 4 inches (10 cm) tall. At first the cap is hemispherical and the young mushrooms are referred to as buttons; they are white or very pale brown, and dry. Later they become convex and finally expanded. They are smooth with a silky texture, and at times slightly scaly; remains of the partial veil often hang fringe-like from the margin. The thin, crowded gills are free. They are pale pink at first, then change through rose-pink to purplish-brown, and finally become black with age. The spores are dark brown. The smooth white stem is stout, rather short, and with a white membranous ring that quickly erodes and falls away; sometimes it tapers towards the base. The flesh is thick and white, becoming pale pink when cut or when infested with insect larvae. It may be eaten cooked or raw, and has a mild flavour. The mushroom so commonly marketed today is a cultivated white form, *alba*, of the wild species *Agaricus bisporus*.

The fine flavour of mushrooms makes this group of fungi the most versatile for culinary purposes. The buttons can be fried in butter or made into mild chutneys; the larger mushrooms are excellent stewed in butter and sprinkled with chopped parsley. They are also useful for soups, sauces and stuffings.

Mushroom purée

1 pint (600 ml) chicken stock
8 oz (250 g) mushrooms
1 onion
2 oz (50 g) butter or margarine
1 oz (25 g) flour
Salt and pepper

Peel and chop the onion and fry gently in 1 oz (25 g) of butter until soft. Add the chicken stock, salt and pepper, and simmer for 15 minutes. Melt the remaining butter and blend in the flour with a wooden spoon to form a smooth paste. Place the mushrooms, the onion mixture and flour mixture into a blender and blend for 15 seconds.

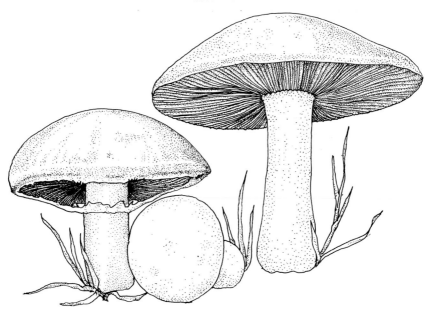

Mushrooms on toast

8 oz (250 g) mushrooms
1 oz (25 g) butter or margarine
Chopped parsley
4 tablespoons cream
Salt and pepper
Toast

Slice the mushrooms and place in a pan with the butter or margarine. Cook gently for 10 minutes, then add the cream, chopped parsley, salt and pepper. Stir until the mixture thickens and serve on toast.

Mushrooms with tomatoes

1 lb (500 g) mushrooms
8 oz (250 g) tomatoes
1 teaspoon chopped onion
1 oz (25 g) parsley
Juice of $\frac{1}{2}$ lemon
$1\frac{1}{2}$ tablespoons olive oil
Salt and pepper

Grease an oven-proof dish well. Peel the mushrooms and chop them coarsely; quarter the tomatoes. Place both mushrooms and tomatoes in the dish and sprinkle them with parsley, onion and lemon juice: season with salt and pepper. Sprinkle the mixture with olive oil and bake in a hot oven for 20 minutes.

Pickled mushrooms

Wash and dry the mushrooms well and remove the stalks. Place them in sterilized jars with a few shallots and bay leaves. Boil some vinegar and pour it over the mushrooms until they are covered. Seal tightly when the vinegar is cold.

Mushroom stuffing

8 oz (250 g) small mushrooms
1 small onion
1 oz (25 g) butter or margarine
4 oz (100 g) breadcrumbs
2 eggs
1 teaspoon grated lemon rind
3 teaspoons lemon juice
$\frac{1}{2}$ teaspoon salt and a pinch of cayenne pepper

Peel and chop the onion and mushrooms and place them in a pan with the butter, salt and pepper: cook until tender. Add the breadcrumbs and mix well over a low heat. Beat the eggs and blend into the mixture, together with the lemon rind and juice. Bind together.

Horse Mushroom
Agaricus arvensis

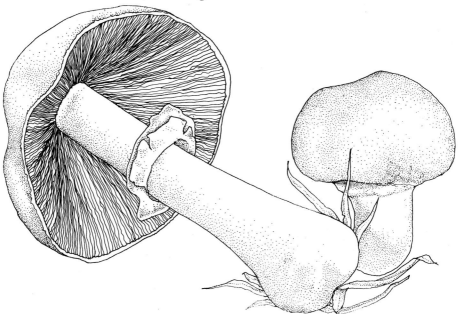

This description should begin with a word of caution. There are two other species which look very like the horse mushroom but can cause sickness if eaten; they are the two yellow-staining mushrooms *Agaricus xanthodermus* and *Agaricus placomyces*. To establish positive identification cut the base of the stem: if there is an immediate colour change to bright yellow it is not the horse mushroom and should not be eaten. July to August are perhaps the best months to find *Agaricus arvensis*. You should look in fields and pastures, particularly where horses have grazed, and it often occurs on roadside verges and occasionally on lawns. It grows up to 8 inches (20 cm) tall and the cap may be of a similar diameter. At first the cap is white and very like a small ball; later it expands, becomes creamy-white and bruises yellowish; it has a kid-glove texture. The gills are free, somewhat crowded and rather narrow. They are greyish at first, turning to pale brown and finally dark brown. The spores are dark purplish-brown. The stem is thick and hollow, and it may or may not be swollen at the base. The lower portion sometimes splits. A broad ring is set high on the stem and often appears to be double. The flesh is thick and firm with a pleasant flavour and an odour of aniseed.

Horse mushrooms are best when picked young as they tend to dry out and become tougher with age. The young buttons can be used in similar preparations to field mushrooms but they require longer cooking. The large mushrooms can be stuffed or grilled, and their strong flavour makes them particularly good when chopped up and used in soups, stews, pies and ketchups.

Mushroom soup

¾ lb (350 g) mushrooms
3 oz (75 g) flour
3 oz (75 g) butter or margarine
1 pint (600 ml) milk
1 pint (600 ml) stock or water
Salt and pepper

Chop the mushrooms finely and fry them in the butter for 5 minutes, stirring to prevent discolouring. Remove the pan from the heat and stir in the flour. Cook for a further 3 minutes. Again remove from the heat and gradually stir in the stock and the milk. Bring to the boil and simmer until the soup thickens. Add salt and pepper according to taste.

Mushroom ketchup

3 lb (1.5 kg) mushrooms
4 oz (100 g) salt
Black pepper
Ginger
All-spice and blades of mace

Break up the mushrooms and place in layers with the salt in a stone jar. Leave for 3 days. Press the mixture well, then cover the jar and place in a cool oven for 2 hours. Strain the liquid through a sieve, pressing to extract all the juice. Boil this juice for 15 minutes and for each pint of liquid (600 ml), add half an ounce (15 g) of black pepper, quarter ounce (10 g) of ginger, a pinch of all-spice and a blade of mace. Boil the mixture rapidly for 30 minutes. When cold, pour into sterilized jars and seal.

Stewed Mushrooms

½ lb (250 g) fresh mushrooms
1 oz (25 g) butter
1 teaspoon chopped parsley
¼ pint (150 ml) tomato or brown sauce
Salt and pepper

Peel the mushrooms and fry in the butter. Add the sauce and simmer gently for 15 minutes. Serve hot with chopped parsley and season with salt and pepper.

Mushroom sauce

2 oz (50 g) mushrooms
1 oz (25 g) butter
1 oz (25 g) flour
½ pint (300 ml) milk
Salt and pepper

Chop the mushrooms and cook in the milk until tender. Strain the mushrooms, keeping the milk for the sauce. Add a quarter of the milk to the flour, salt and pepper and mix with a wooden spoon to a smooth paste. Bring the remaining milk to the boil and gradually add the flour mixture, stirring all the time. Place the sauce on a low heat and stir until it boils. Maintain the stirring and simmer for a further 3 minutes. Add the butter and the mushrooms and reheat.

Fennel
Foeniculum vulgare

Fennel is an herbaceous perennial of erect habit, to be found especially on sea cliffs growing alongside Sea Thrift and Sea Lavender, or in the sandy soil at the foot of the cliffs with the Sandworts. It is often found in quantity on some salt marshes. It grows to heights of 3 to 5 feet (90 to 150 cm); the stems are branching, round below, are finely furrowed and polished, either filled with pith or solid. The leaves are dark green, and twice ternate. The leaflets are pinnatifid (feather-like). In July and August it produces many tiny yellow flowers, which are borne in smallish concave umbels. The fruit is egg-shaped. Although fennel is plentiful and appears to be entirely wild, many botanists do not consider it to be truly indigenous. Remembering how in days gone by it was grown in so very many kitchen gardens throughout the country the chances are that it has become naturalized over the years rather than being a native.

This distinctive herb has a fresh nutty flavour and a scent of new-mown hay. Although all parts of the plant are edible, the thinner stems, leaves and seeds are most useful. The leaves should be picked between July and September and can be used fresh or dried; the seeds should be collected between September and October and must be under-ripe and pale green in colour; the roots should be unearthed between March and April.

The young stems can be chopped raw in salads, or boiled and eaten as a vegetable. The finely chopped leaves are used for flavouring sauces, vegetable salads and soups; they are especially useful in the preparation of fish dishes, particularly when served with boiled mackerel.

The seeds give added flavour when cooked with beef stew, roast pork, apples and boiled fish, and together with the newly opened flowers are used in cucumber pickling. The oil extracted from the herb is employed in making confectionery, cordials and liqueurs; whereas the root can be grated and mixed with breakfast cereal to make a good laxative.

Fennel aids digestion, is one of the ingredients of babies' gripe water and is said to be a cure for bad breath. The seeds are a cure for colic and flatulence and, in the old days, it seems they were boiled in wine and given as a relief to those having eaten poisonous mushrooms. Herbalists recommend the root to be boiled in milk and used as a tonic.

Fennel sauce

3 tablespoons finely chopped fennel
2 tablespoons butter
$3\frac{1}{2}$ tablespoons flour
1 tablespoon vinegar
3 teaspoons sugar
Yolk of an egg
$1\frac{3}{4}$ cups warm stock
Salt and pepper

Melt the butter in a pan and stir in the flour. Gradually blend in the stock to form a smooth paste. Mix in all the remaining ingredients except the egg yolk, and cook gently for 10 minutes. Beat the egg yolk and fold into the mixture. Reheat for a further 5 minutes. Fennel sauce is excellent served with boiled fish.

Fennel leaf wine

2 pints (1200 ml) fennel leaves
1 pint (600 ml) unsweetened grapefruit juice
3½ lb (1.75 kg) sugar
7 pints (4 l) water
¼ teaspoon wine tannin
Yeast and nutrient

Briefly bring the water to the boil whilst stirring in the sugar. Pour over the leaves, cover and allow to cool to room temperature. Stir in the grapefruit juice, tannin, yeast and nutrient. Leave covered for a further week before straining into a fermenting jar and fitting an air-lock. Rack for the first time when the wine clears and bottle after about 6 months.

Tansy
Chrysanthemum vulgare

Tansy grows in bushy clumps some 2 to 3 feet (60 to 90 cm) tall; it is a sand-loving, herbaceous perennial and likes a dry sunny habitat. It often grows in profusion on banks by the sea, or along the shores of rivers; it is sometimes found along roadsides or hedgerows, and also in cornfields where it may be difficult to eradicate. It is often cultivated in gardens. Its stiff upright stems are usually simple, angular and grooved. The leaves are composed of several leaflets, each deeply cut into many fine segments, the margin of each segment being itself serrated. The surface of these dark green leaves bears innumerable glands containing an aromatic oil; under a lens they appear as a series of dots. Not until August and September do we find it in flower. The flowers are borne in flat-topped, terminal corymbs comprising up to forty or more golden yellow, buttonlike, blooms; each consisting of about 400 tiny perfect flowers, tightly packed in rings, and held in a cup of green bracts (the involucre). The florets mature from the outer ring inwards, as is usual in this family. Its fruit is a hard, dry, single-seeded object (an achene) with a membrane that helps in some way towards its dispersal by the wind.

Tanacetum, a former Latin name, means literally 'a bed of tansy'. The common name tansy is a corruption of the Greek word *thanatos*, 'death'. Other common names include 'Bachelor's Buttons', 'Ginger Plant' and 'Bitter Buttons'.

A green dye can be extracted from its roots and it was once very much used in Finland for dyeing cloth. Tansy derives its scent and flavour from essential oils, which though beneficial in small quantities can be a considerable irritant to the stomach if taken in excess. The young, finely shredded leaves add seasoning and

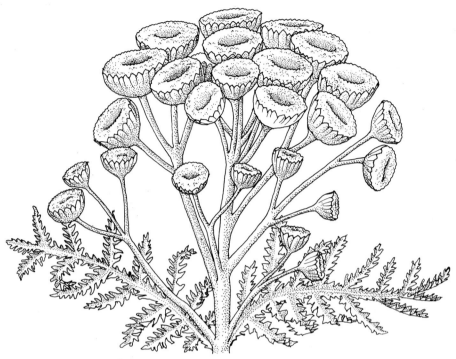

colouring to cakes, omelettes and puddings; 'tansy cakes', made from young leaves and eggs, were once eaten at Easter as a symbol of the bitter herbs taken by the Jews at the Passover. The leaves are also used to make a tea which is useful as a spring tonic: pour 1 pint (600 ml) of boiling water over a heaped tablespoon of dried leaves and infuse for a few minutes before straining. The tea should be drunk a cupful at a time and although it once expelled worms in children it is also valuable in treating hysteria, nausea and kidney weakness. The root, preserved in sugar or honey, was eaten during a period of strict dieting as a cure for gout.

Sea Lettuce or Green Laver
Ulva lactuca

Of all the green seaweeds this is the most conspicuous, and often forms the largest exposed masses of vegetable growth between the tide marks. It occurs in all the shore zones except the uppermost reaches of the beach, and is common on most rocky shores and mudflats, especially where the land creates sheltered bays; it is also found in pools, and is tolerant of freshwater. In areas where untreated sewage is released into the sea its prolific growth can only be regarded as a nuisance. July and August are the months when it is particularly abundant. Its thin, flat green fronds grow in bunches, are of irregular shape, and occasionally as broad as they are long. The

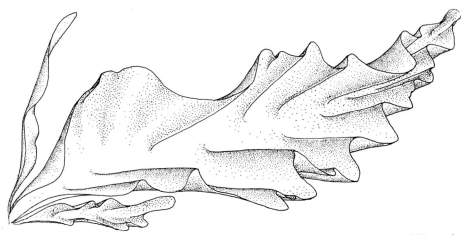

margin is wavy, and the stipe which is always present is secured by a holdfast of very small viscose threads. The usual length is from 4 to 8 inches (10 to 20 cm), but at times it reaches 18 inches (45 cm), and twice this length in the USA. When young the fronds are pale green, then bright green in maturity, and finally dark green with age. The margins of mature fronds may appear whitish after the release of spores. In water the fronds bear a strong resemblance to limp leaves of lettuce, hence the common name. Seaweeds are a source of food for the molluscs, and the sea-hare (*Aplysia punctata*) which is a herbivore apparently depends on the sea lettuce as its main source of food. The worldwide distribution of this common weed includes Europe, India, Australia and the USA. Seaweed makes an excellent organic manure, and may be used as an alternative to the more usual farmyard product. Although rich in potash it is as a rule comparatively low in phosphates and nitrogen (but Sea Lettuce which has been growing in waters contaminated by sewage is also rich in nitrogen).

When picked from the most unpolluted shores and thoroughly washed it can be eaten raw sprinkled with lemon juice as part of a salad. Alternatively it can be boiled in salt water for 20 minutes, then strained and chopped. The pulpy mass which results can be served as a vegetable sprinkled with lemon juice or vinegar and is delicious with macaroni cheese or boiled brown rice. It can be used in similar ways to laver seaweed but the results are not as good.

Green Laver (Sea Lettuce) sauce

2 cups boiled sea lettuce
1 oz (25 g) butter
Juice of $\frac{1}{2}$ lemon

Rinse the sea lettuce thoroughly under the tap to remove all sand and mud particles; then simmer gently until soft and mushy. Measure 2 cups of the seaweed and mix in the butter and lemon juice. Beat the sauce well with a fork and serve hot with mutton.

Autumn

Hop
Humulus lupulus

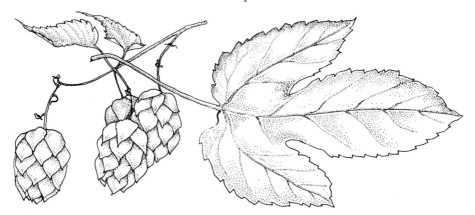

The indigenous wild hop is a lover of rich marshy woodlands and copses, but the ground must not be too damp; it also requires warmth and sunshine. Its shoots are not sufficiently rigid to give the plant an erect habit. Without support it would lie prostrate on the ground and in all probability perish—hence the generic name *Humulus* from the Latin *humus*, meaning 'ground' (or it may allude to the humus soil enjoyed by the hop). However, within its habitat it does find ample support in the form of bushes, small trees, and hedges, upon which it readily attaches itself by virtue of the 6 longitudinal rows of tiny anvil-shaped hooks along the stem; the hooks are most numerous immediately below the flowers. As the stem pushes forward so the hooks engage into the support plant. The hop also has a twining growth, revolving in a clockwise direction, and each complete revolution of the tip is said to take 2 hours. It grows to heights or lengths of 4 to 12 feet (1.25 to 3.5 metres). The leaves are palmate with 3 to 5 lobes (3 are very distinct and egg-shaped, the other 2 somewhat smaller), and serrated at the margin. They are stalked, opposite, smooth above, rough below and distinctly veined.

Flowering occurs from July to September. The male plants bear yellowish-green flowers, $\frac{1}{4}$ inch (6 mm) across, in loose clusters several inches long, and each flower has 5 sepals which in appearance resemble a star. In contrast the female plants bear very tiny flowers, many of which are gathered together to form rounded heads, referred to as 'catkins' or 'cones', the flower-stalk rising at the angle between the leaf-stem and the branch. Each 'cone' comprises a number of triangular, pointed green bracts (these are crowded together around a central axis). Each bract surrounds 2 female flowers, and each flower consists of a single sepal and an ovary. The male flowers soon wither and die after the wind has blown away their pollen and so fertilized the females. During September and October the scent of the hop is unequalled by the briar rose, honeysuckle, or the lavender. When the female 'cones' eventually dry and break up, so the wind disperses the seeds with the sepals acting like small sails. Within the sail are fine grains of a strong-smelling and equally strong-tasting substance known as 'lupuline', hence the specific name *lupulus*.

Lupuline not only deters the birds from eating the seeds, but is also the substance which gives the bitter taste to beer as well as aiding the clearing process and improving its keeping qualities. Hop flowers can be used to flavour home-brewed ales. Fresh flowers impart the stronger flavour, but for a lighter brew dry them first at no more than 26°C (80°F).

Young hop shoots can be picked in spring, tied in bundles and boiled for 20 minutes to be eaten as a vegetable in the same way as asparagus. They can also be used in soups or chopped with butter in a sauce. A tea made from the plant is brewed by simmering a handful of dried hops in 0.5 litre (just under a pint) of water for 5 minutes. It is said to be an inducement to sleep, as well as a tonic, an aid to digestion and a mild narcotic (it belongs to the same botanical family as cannabis). Pillows stuffed with hops act as a sedative and are still used by some people who suffer from insomnia.

Hop wine

4 oz (100 g) hops
3 lb (1.5 kg) sugar
7 pints (4 l) water
1 oz (25 g) bruised ginger
Juice of 1 orange
Juice of 1 lemon
Yeast and nutrient

Simmer the hops and ginger in the water for an hour. Strain, then add the fruit juice and sugar to the liquid, stirring well to dissolve all the sugar. When it has cooled to room temperature add the yeast and nutrient. Pour into a fermenting jar and fit an air-lock. Rack when the wine clears and bottle after about 6 months.

Dog Rose
Rosa canina

The dog rose is a large, climbing, deciduous, perennial shrub with long spreading branches bearing wicked thorns; the branches are arched and the plant attains heights of between 8 and 10 feet (2.5 and 3 metres). It is a humous-loving plant requiring a sandy loam. Its leaves are pinnate, with simply-toothed and hairless leaflets. Flowering is continuous from June to July, but seldom into the last week of the latter month. Each flower has 5 pink and white petals, and 5 sharply pointed green sepals, but alas lives for only two days from the bud opening. For one night the petals close to protect the yellow stamens from the rain and dew; on the following day when the pollen is gone and the rose's life virtually over there is no further need for those delicate petals to give protection. Although the dog rose produces abundant pollen, it is devoid of nectar.

The various scents of wild roses are very distinct, and it is probably quite possible for a blind person to determine the species by smell alone. Our rosehip is actually a false fruit, for it is really only the stalk end; the true fruits, which each contain one seed, are the tiny hairy objects within it. To countryfolk it is also known as the 'Canker Rose', so called no doubt because of the numerous galls with a moss-like covering one often sees on its leaves. These are caused by the rose-gall wasp *Rhodites rosae* which lays her eggs in the leaf buds; on hatching the tiny larvae creep further into the leaf tissue and hence galls are formed. They are also known as 'bedeguars' or 'Robins' Cushions'. Perhaps the most generally accepted theory for the derivation of the name dog rose is founded on an ancient belief that the root was cure for the bite of a mad dog; but more probably it was originally called the 'Dag Rose', 'dag' being short for dagger and alluding to its dagger-like thorns.

In generations past a conserve of rose was used for cooling the 'heate of the eye', and in Chaucer's time the petals were used on wounds and in ointments.

The importance of rosehips as a valuable source of vitamin C was recognized in the Second World War when volunteers were set the task of collecting the hips to make the syrup. During the war years, some $2\frac{1}{2}$ million bottles of home-made syrup were produced. The wild rosehip is still collected today to provide the raw material for the syrup produced by manufacturers. In fact, collecting rosehips is still a valuable source of income for some northern schools, where the pupils between them gather hundreds of pounds of hips in a season, and are paid a few pence per pound by the manufacturers for their harvest.

The hips should be picked in October after the first frost has softened them. The seeds are covered in dangerous hairs, which are best removed along with the seeds, leaving the fleshy part for use. However, this is not absolutely necessary when making rosehip jelly, syrup or wine, since fine nylon jelly-bags or sieves are used to separate liquid from solid.

Rosehip and Crab Apple jelly

2 lb (1 kg) rosehips
5 lb (2.5 kg) crab apples
3 pints (1800 ml) water
Sugar

Wash the crabs, slice (no need to peel and core) and place in a pan with $1\frac{1}{2}$ pints (900 ml) of water. Simmer the apples to a pulp. Mince the rosehips in a coarse mincer and simmer separately with the remaining $1\frac{1}{2}$ pints of water for 10 minutes and allow to stand for a further 10 minutes. Strain the two mixtures together through a jelly-bag overnight. Measure the juice and allow 1 lb of sugar for each pint of juice. Bring the liquid to the boil, add the warmed sugar and stir until dissolved. Boil rapidly until the jelly sets when tested. Follow the standard procedure set out in the Introduction.

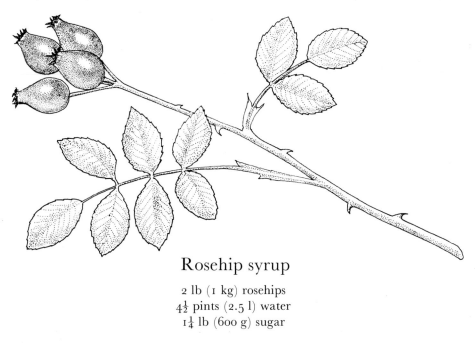

Rosehip syrup

2 lb (1 kg) rosehips
$4\frac{1}{2}$ pints (2.5 l) water
$1\frac{1}{4}$ lb (600 g) sugar

Mince the fruit in a coarse mincer and place immediately in 3 pints (1800 ml) of boiling water. Bring the mixture back to the boil and then remove from the heat for 15 minutes. Strain through a fine jelly-bag. Place the pulp mixture in the pan and add a further $1\frac{1}{2}$ pints (900 ml) of boiling water. Stir and allow the mixture to stand for 10 minutes, then strain through the jelly-bag overnight. Wash the pan thoroughly, then place in it the strained liquid and boil the juice until it is reduced to about $1\frac{1}{2}$ pints (900 ml). Add the warmed sugar, stir until dissolved and boil for 5 minutes. Pour the syrup while still hot into warm, sterilized bottles and seal immediately.

Rosehip sauce

$\frac{3}{4}$ pint (450 ml) water
$\frac{1}{2}$ lb (250 g) rosehips
$\frac{1}{2}$ tablespoon cornflour
1 teaspoon lemon juice
4 tablespoons sugar

Cut the hips in half and remove the inner seeds. Place the outer flesh in the water and bring to the boil. Cover and simmer gently for $1\frac{1}{2}$ hours, or until tender. Sieve, forcing as much pulp through as possible. Return to the pan and reheat. Mix the cornflour in a little water and add to the liquid; stir until the mixture thickens and add the sugar and lemon juice. This is excellent when served with asparagus or broccoli.

Rosehip wine

3 lb (1.5 kg) rosehips
3 lb (1.5 kg) sugar
7 pints (4 l) water
1 teaspoon citric acid
Pectic enzyme
Yeast and nutrient

Wash the hips well and slice in half. Crush them with a wooden mallet and add to the sugar. Pour on the boiling water and stir well to dissolve all the sugar. Allow to cool to about 20°C before adding the acid, enzyme, yeast and nutrient. Cover closely and leave in a warm place for 2 weeks, stirring daily. Strain through fine nylon netting into a dark fermenting jar and fit an air-lock. Rack for the first time when the wine clears.

Juniper
Juniperus communis

In Britain the juniper occurs chiefly as spreading, low-growing, and usually untidy evergreen shrub, 20 to 60 inches (0.5 to 1.5 metres) tall, and locally common in open chalky places on hill sides and sea cliffs. The species is very variable in both size and form, depending to a great extent on its location; at times it may grow as a small narrow tree of 10 to 20 feet (3 to 6 metres) tall. The fibrous bark is flaky and varies in colour from dark brown to reddish brown. Its leaves are linear, about ¾ inch (2 cm) long, sharply pointed, rigid, thick at the margin, and without a stalk; they grow in whorls of three around the branches. The upper side is concave, and green with a broad longitudinal glaucous band; the underside is entirely green. Male and female flowers occur on separate trees and are produced during May. The male catkins are bud-like and have numerous anthers which are yellow with pollen. The tiny female flowers resemble small buds and can be found in the leaf axils. It is not until September or October of the second year that the small, globular, cone-like berries ripen to bluish-black; the first-year berries are still green at that time. The ripe fruit is spongy and very pungent but not juicy. Each contains 3 oblong seeds. Juniper berries are used to flavour certain food dishes, including the meats of game.

The berries should first be dried before use. Pick them when they are mature and dry them slowly until they turn blackish, when they can be stored until required. A few crushed berries impart a good flavour to stuffings and forcemeat and they are sometimes used in spice pickles. They can also be distilled to make oil of juniper. Gins were formerly flavoured with them, and as the berries have long been regarded as a kidney stimulant the gin drinker was provided with adequate justification.

The berries contain vitamin C and a few crushed berries make a fine herbal tea which will sooth urinary discomfort. They are also an abortifacient, however, and one of the plant's most common names is 'kill-bastard'.

Juniper wood is aromatic and is burnt along with other woods to cure certain fish in some countries. It is capable of taking a high polish and so is used by turners to make many small articles.

Juniper sauce

4 crushed juniper berries
4 tablespoons butter
3 tablespoons finely chopped onion
3 teaspoons lemon juice
1 tablespoon chopped parsley
Salt and pepper

Melt the butter, add the onion and cook until soft. Remove from the heat and stir in the crushed juniper berries, lemon juice and parsley. Season with salt and pepper. Juniper sauce is excellent served over baked potatoes.

Sloe or Blackthorn
Prunus spinosa

It derives the name blackthorn from its black bark which distinguishes it from the hawthorn. During March, April and early May the white flowers (not unlike hawthorn blossom) bloom in profusion and regularly appear long before the bush comes into leaf. It grows wild throughout the British Isles and Europe with the exception of the most northerly regions. The blackthorn often produces a great number of suckers, whereby a single bush may, over the years, develop into a small thicket. It produces an almost impenetrable barrier and is often grown as a field hedge. The leaves are small, about 3 cm long, dull green and finely toothed. Sloe berries are fully grown by September but green, and do not mature until late October and early November when they are seen as a round fruit, half an inch (13 mm) in diameter, of bluish-black and with a delicate bloom. Their tannin content gives them a very sour taste. As protection from the long pointed thorns many people prefer to wear gloves when picking sloes.

The first frost makes the skins softer and more permeable, and the sloes are best picked immediately after this. The leaves and flowers can be made into a tea which has diuretic and laxative properties, whereas the fruits are used by herbalists to make stomach tonics and syrups containing vitamin C.

Sloe jam

4 lb (2 kg) sloes
6 lb (3 kg) sugar
1½ pints (900 ml) water

Wash the sloes and place in a preserving pan with the water; bring to the boil and simmer for 30 minutes. Add the warmed sugar and stir until completely dissolved. Boil rapidly until the jam sets when tested (approximately 10 minutes). Most stones can be skimmed from the top of the jam when boiling. Follow the standard procedure.

Sloe jelly

6 lb (3 kg) sloes
4 pints (2.5 l) water
1½ lb (750 g) sugar
Juice of 4 oranges

Wash and dry the sloes and place in a preserving pan with the water. Simmer for 2 hours and then strain through a jelly-bag overnight. Reheat the liquid and add the warmed sugar and orange juice. Stir over a low heat until the sugar is dissolved, then boil rapidly until the jelly sets when tested (approximately 15 minutes). Follow the standard procedure. Sloe jelly is excellent served with mutton, game or veal.

Sloe wine

3 lb (1.5 kg) sloes
¼ pint (150 ml) red grape concentrate
3 lb (1.5 kg) sugar
7 pints (4 l) water
Pectic enzyme
Yeast and nutrient

Pour the boiling water over the sloes and mash them well. Add the grape concentrate and 2 lb (1 kg) of the sugar; stir well. When it has cooled to room temperature, add the pectic enzyme, and a day later stir in the yeast and nutrient. Cover well and leave in a warm place for 8 days, stirring daily. Strain through a nylon sieve and stir in the remaining sugar. Pour into a fermenting jar and fit an air-lock. Leave to ferment for a month in a warm place.

A little more sugar can be added at this stage, if a sweeter wine is required. Rack, and allow the fermentation to continue in a cooler place. Bottle when the wine has cleared, but this wine is better if left for at least a year before drinking.

Sloe gin

Sloes
Castor sugar
Gin
Almond essence

Wipe the sloes clean and prick them with a needle. Half fill a Kilner jar with the sloes and add the same weight of castor sugar. Fill the jar up to the top with gin and screw down tightly. Shake and turn the jar upside down regularly over the next few weeks to dissolve all the sugar. Add a few drops of almond essence and, after capping firmly again, leave in a reasonable warm place for 10 weeks, shaking occasionally. Strain several times through fine nylon netting and bottle.

Wild Harvest jam

1 lb (500 g) blackberries
1 lb (500 g) elderberries
1 lb (500 g) crab apples
8 oz (250 g) sloes
3 pints (1800 ml) water
3½ lb (1.75 kg) sugar

Wash and dry all the fruit; peel and core the crabs; remove the stalks from the sloes and prick them with a needle. Place all the fruit in a preserving pan with the water and simmer until soft, removing as many of the sloe stones as possible during cooking. Stir in the warmed sugar until dissolved, then boil rapidly until the jam sets when tested. Follow the standard procedure on jam-making.

Crab Apple
Malus sylvestris

The crab apple is a lover of clay or sandy soils, and may be found growing in woodlands and copses; also in hedgerows when it is difficult to determine if it really is wild or just a reversion to type of some orchard apple. It grows to about 20 or 25 feet (6 or 7.5 metres) tall; just a small tree with numerous, repeatedly divided, branches that spread widely when young, drooping in later years. Sometimes it only attains the proportions of a bush, when the diameter of spread by its lower branches is often greater in dimension than its height. The bark is greyish-brown in colour, and

although numerously fissured not very rough. The leaves are borne on long slender stalks, they are more or less broadly oval with a sharp tip, and serrated margin; their upper surface smooth, the underside often downy when young. It flowers profusely during April and May, producing flowers in clusters, each one lasting for 5 to 6 days. They are large, white and tinged with pink; and early in the flowering season many are still attendant as deep pink buds. There are 5 united sepals which are hairy above, 5 pink and white petals, 5 stigmas, and numerous stamens. Because their scent is stronger at night time the chief insect visitors are nocturnal moths which alight to feed on the nectar. After fertilization the ovary and receptacle-walls begin to swell, eventually becoming a fleshy and juicy fruit with a persistent calyx above. The typical form of crab apple is a small yellow pome flushed with red, about 1 inch (25 mm) in diameter, and its juice so sour as to curdle milk. There are of course many varieties, one with fruit little bigger than a cherry.

The juice of the crab is called 'verjuice' or 'vargis', and in Ireland this was put in cider to make it rough; the juice has also been used to treat sprains and bruises. An ointment for curing burns was made from verjuice and 'hard yeast'. Pigs seem very fond of eating crabs, perhaps an inheritance from the wild boar. Over the years the crab apple tree has proved of great horticultural value as a stock on which other varieties might be grafted. *Malus* is the Latin for apple, and *sylvestris* refers to its woodland habitat. The name crab is thought by some to be a form of the Lowland Scotch *scrab* which is derived from *scrobb*, the Anglo-Saxon word for a shrub; indicating that it is not really a tree but a bush. Other common names include Apple-John, Crab-stock, Morris Apple, Scarb Jacket and Scrog.

Crab Apple jelly

6 lb (3 kg) crab apples
3½ pints (2 l) water
Juice of 1 lemon
Sugar

Wipe and slice the apples (there is no need to peel and core) and place in a pan with the water. Simmer the fruit until soft and pulpy and then strain overnight through a jelly-bag. Measure the liquid and for each pint allow 1 pound (500 g) of sugar. Add the lemon juice, bring the liquid to the boil and stir in the warmed sugar until dissolved. Boil rapidly until the jelly sets when tested (approximately 15 minutes). Remove the scum and follow the standard procedure.

Crab Apple and Blackberry pudding

8 oz (250 g) ripe crab apples
1 lb (500 g) blackberries
8 oz (250 g) sugar
1 small stale loaf of bread
½ pint (300 ml) water

Peel, core and slice the apples and simmer with the blackberries in the water for 10 minutes. Drain off the water and add the sugar to the fruit. Cut the bread into thick slices, remove the crusts and line the sides and bottom of a deep pudding basin with the bread so that the slices overlap. Keep aside a layer of bread for the top of the pudding. Place the fruit mixture in the basin and cover the top with the remaining slices of bread. Place a saucer on top with a heavy weight and leave in a refrigerator overnight. The pudding is best served chilled with cream.

Crab Apple and Rowanberry jelly

1 lb (500 g) crab apples
1½ lb (750 g) rowanberries
Juice of 1 lemon
1 pint (600 ml) water
Sugar

Slice the crab apples (there is no need to peel and core) and place in a pan with the rowanberries and water. Simmer until the fruit is soft (at least an hour) and strain overnight through a jelly-bag. Measure the liquid and for each pint allow 1¼ lb (600 g) of sugar. Bring the liquid back to the boil and add the lemon juice and the warmed sugar. Stir until the sugar is dissolved and boil rapidly until the jelly sets when tested (about 10 minutes). Remove the scum and follow the standard procedure.

Crab Apple and Sloe jelly

5 lb (2.5 kg) crab apples
2 lb (1 kg) sloes
2 pints (1200 ml) water
Sugar

Slice the crab apples (no need to peel and core) and place in the preserving pan with the sloes and water. Simmer until the fruit is pulpy, then strain through a jelly-bag overnight. Measure the liquid and for each pint allow 1 lb (500 g) of sugar. Bring the liquid to the boil, remove from the heat source and stir in the warmed sugar until it has been dissolved. Boil rapidly until the jelly sets when tested. Skim off the scum and follow the standard procedure for jelly-making. This jelly makes an excellent accompaniment to mutton or rabbit.

Crab Apple wine

5 lb (2.5 kg) crab apples
3 lb (1.5 kg) sugar
$\frac{1}{4}$ pint (150 ml) white grape concentrate
7 pints (4 l) water
1 lemon
Yeast and nutrient

Cut up the whole apples and simmer for 15 minutes in the water. Strain through a nylon sieve onto the sugar and thinly peeled rind of the lemon. Stir well to dissolve all the sugar. Allow to cool to room temperature (70°F, 21°C) before adding the lemon juice, grape concentrate, yeast and nutrient. Cover well and leave for 24 hours in a warm place. Then pour the liquid into a fermenting jar and fit an air-lock. Rack after the initial fermentation has subsided and do not bottle for at least 6 months.

<u>Hazel</u>
Corylus avellana

Hedges, copses and woods are the habitat of the hazel, which grows usually as a coppiced bush or a small tree, attaining heights of 15 to 20 feet (4.5 to 6 metres). The thin bark is smooth, silvery greyish-brown, is often peeling away, and is punctated with numerous light coloured lenticels. It is deciduous and flourishes only in a good soil, although it will grow almost anywhere. The flowers mature during late January and February; the pendulous male catkins, or 'lambs' tails', as they are commonly referred to, hang in small clusters and are at first pale green, later becoming bright yellow with pollen. They vary in length from 1 to 3 inches (2 to 7 cm).

The female flowers are very small, less than $\frac{1}{4}$ inch (5 mm) across, and only seen after close inspection; they are like tiny swollen buds with little crimson clusters of fine threads protruding (these are the styles and stigmas). It is not until late April

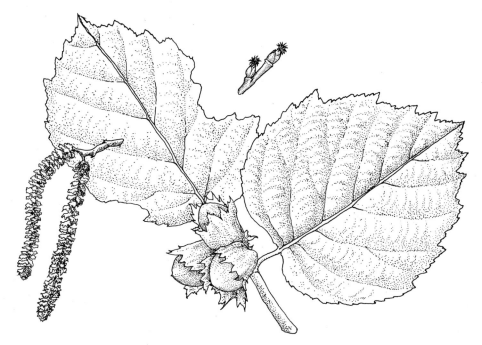

and May that the leaves open. They are roundish heart-shaped, pointed at the tip, doubly serrated, and downy beneath, 2 to 4 inches (5 to 10 cm) long. The petiole is short and stout. By October each of the fertile female flowers has developed into a cluster of one to four nuts, which are surrounded by the leathery, enlarged and ragged-edged bracts. The shell is the ovary that has now become hard and woody. The word hazelnut comes from the Anglo-Saxon *haselnutu*, *hasel* 'a cup', and *knutu* 'a nut'. Its timber has in the past been used for making walking-sticks, thatching rods, and hurdles. Forked hazel switches are used as dowsing rods to locate the position of water, or a mineral lode.

The best time to gather the nuts is when they are turning brown, usually towards the end of September. They are ripe if they fall from their husks when the tree is shaken. Store the nuts in their shells in a cool dry place until they are required.

Hazelnuts are the most common nuts to be found in this country and are the most valuable nutritionally. They are rich in vitamins B1 and C, and calcium and their protein, mineral and fat content compares favourably with eggs and milk. Eat the whole shelled nuts raw or chop them as an addition to muesli and salads or as a good substitute for almonds. A delicious nutritional drink can be made by using 1 part shelled hazelnuts to 1 part honey and 3 parts milk. The nuts should be finely ground and then blended with the milk and honey.

Hazelnut spread

6 oz (150 g) hazelnut kernels
1 lb (500 g) butter

Blanch the kernels in boiling water, then crush until a smooth paste is obtained (sprinkle with a little water to help the process). Cream the nuts with the butter and finally press through a sieve. The spread is excellent for sandwiches and keeps well in air-tight containers.

Hazelnut meringue

4 oz (100 g) chopped hazelnuts
3 oz (75 g) castor sugar
3 oz (75 g) icing sugar
Whites of 3 eggs
Pinch of salt

Mix the hazelnuts, castor and icing sugar together and add a pinch of salt. Fold this into the whisked egg whites and place in a well-buttered oven-proof dish. Position this in the centre of the oven and bake at 225°F (107°C) for 2½ hours until the meringue is crisp.

Sweet or Spanish Chestnut
Castanea sativa

A truly magnificent tree, sturdy and with a broad crown. It occasionally attains a height of 100 feet (31 metres) and often has a girth of 40 feet (12.5 metres). It was probably introduced to Britain by the Romans, but as far as Europe is concerned it is indigenous only to the southern and eastern parts. The leaves are some 10 inches (25 cm) in length, shaped like the blade of a spear and boldly toothed at the margin. Flowering occurs in June and July when male catkins are produced along erect stalks, with the green female bud-like flowers positioned at the base of the stalk in groups of three. Only in the southern counties of Britain can we hope to find chestnuts of any size, Italy being the country of origin for many of our eating chestnuts. The fertile female flowers are quick to mature when the familiar spiny cups containing the shiny brown nuts begin to appear. These fall to the ground during late October and November, so releasing the nuts.

They are then ready to eat and it seems a task to remove the nuts from their spiny seed coverings; nevertheless, their delicious taste makes it well worthwhile. Chestnuts have a good mineral content as well as vitamins B and C, and are less oily and more digestible than other nuts. When eaten raw, they are crisp and enjoyable, but the slightly bitter inner skin should be removed first. The raw nuts will not keep

Shaggy Caps
Coprinus comatus

Sloes
Prunus spinosa

Rosehips
Rosa canina

Jew's Ear Fungus
Hirneola auricula-judae

Wood Blewits
Lepista nuda

Hops
Humulus lupulus

Parasol Mushroom
Lepiota procera

Saffron Milk Cap
Lactarius deliciosus

Hazel
Corylus avellana

Crab Apple
Malus sylvestris

Mussels
Mytilus edulis

Common Periwinkle
Littorina littorea

Edible Cockles
Cardium edule

Laver Seaweed
Porphyra umbilicalis

Juniper berries
Juniperus communis

Walnut
Juglans regia

Rowan
Sorbus aucuparia

Sweet Chestnut
Castanea sativa

longer than two months but they can be dried after shelling; if required at a later date, they can be reconstituted by soaking in water. Chestnuts can be roasted—do not peel them, just slit the skins and place in the hot ash of the fire or very close to the fire itself. To test when they are ready to eat, an old recipe book suggests placing one un-slit nut with the others—when this bursts, they should all be well roasted. Remove the peel before eating. Do not confuse with the conkers of the Common Horse Chestnut.

When boiling chestnuts, place in a pan, cover with water and boil until they are soft. Peel off the skins with a sharp knife whilst they are hot.

In the past, the nuts have been ground into flour and then used in cakes, bread, soups and stews. They can be pickled in vinegar, preserved in sugar or syrup and also puréed. Chestnut stuffing can be made from the finely chopped nuts and is used traditionally for stuffing the Christmas turkey.

Sweet Chestnut soup

1 lb (500 g) chestnuts
2 oz (50 g) butter or margarine
1 pint (600 ml) white stock or water
½ pint (300 ml) milk
Salt and pepper

Wipe the chestnuts and split the skins. Place in a pan, cover with water or stock and cook for 15 minutes. Remove the skins from the nuts while hot, then return the chestnuts to the water or stock and simmer for 45 minutes. Rub the softened nuts through a sieve and then place all the ingredients in a pan and heat slowly.

Turkey stuffing

8 oz (250 g) chestnuts
2 oz (50 g) breadcrumbs
1 oz (25 g) grated suet
1 tablespoon chopped parsley
1 tablespoon lemon juice
1 egg
Pinch of salt

With a sharp knife, slit the skins of the chestnuts and boil in water for 30 minutes. Drain off the water and remove the skins while hot. Rub through a sieve and mix well with the breadcrumbs, suet, parsley, lemon juice and salt. Bind together with the beaten egg.

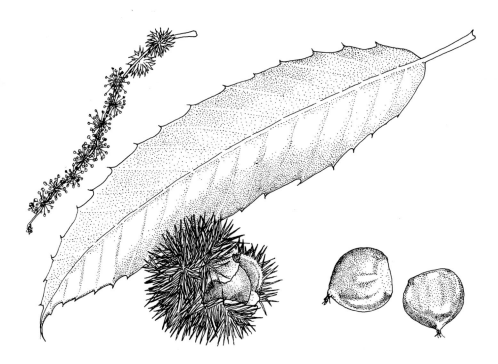

Candied Chestnuts

1 pint (600 ml) sweet chestnuts
1 cup sugar
½ cup water
1 tablespoon rum
Cocktail sticks

Cook the whole peeled chestnuts in boiling water until tender, and then into each one insert a cocktail stick. Place the sugar and water in a pan and heat, stirring continuously until dissolved. Add the rum and continue to boil until the syrup forms a hard ball if a little is dropped into a cup of cold water. Coat the chestnuts all over in the syrup mixture and allow to cool.

Boiled Chestnuts

¾ lb (350 g) chestnuts
½ pint (300 ml) vegetable stock
½ teaspoon salt

Peel the chestnuts and place in a pan with the hot vegetable stock and salt. Simmer · until the stock is absorbed and the nuts are tender (between 20 and 40 minutes). Serve with sprouts or other vegetables.

Roasted Chestnuts

8 oz (250 g) chestnuts
1 lb (500 g) salt
Butter

Cover the roasting tray with a third of the salt. Wipe the chestnuts clean, split the shells with a knife, place them on the tray, then cover with the rest of the salt. Roast in a moderately hot oven for 25 minutes. Put the roasted nuts on a dish and serve with butter. (The salt can be kept and used several times.)

Rowan or Mountain Ash
Sorbus aucuparia

The natural home of the mountain ash is wooded hillsides. It is a rock-loving, deciduous tree, and one of the commonest to be planted along our roadsides and in small suburban gardens. It has an erect habit, and a clean bole whose numerous branches have a tendency to arch upwardly; the average height is between 20 and 40 feet (6 and 12 metres). The smooth, shiny grey bark carries many horizontal linear scars. During April the rowan's leaves begin to unfold. They are pinnate with 6 or 8 pairs of lanceolate leaflets and a terminal one; these have a toothed margin, except towards the base. The upper surface is deep green and smooth, the underside is much paler, and at first downy. In May and June the creamy-white bisexual flowers come into bloom. They are borne terminally on short leafy branches, in dense woolly-stemmed clusters of some 4 to 6 inches (12 to 18 cm) across, and look very much like miniature hawthorn blossom. As the petals fall from the fertile flowers so the fruit begins to form, ripening from tiny green berry-like pomes $\frac{1}{4}$ inch (6 mm) across to become bright scarlet by August and September, and hanging in heavy clusters. Their soft orange flesh is much enjoyed by birds who quickly and methodically strip the tree of its fruit.

The name mountain ash would suggest some relationship with the common ash, but this is not so. The only similarity seems to be the shape of their leaves. The specific name *aucuparia* is from the Latin *auceps*, a 'fowler'; the common name rowan is from the Norse *raun*. Other common names include Fowler's Service, from *cerevisa*, 'a fermented drink'; Cock-drunks and Hen-drunks, because it was thought that fowl were intoxicated if they ate the berries; Witch-wood and Witchen, because of some virtue against witchcraft that it was believed to possess; and Quickbeam, because of the almost perpetual movement of its foliage (this is derived from the Anglo-Saxon *cwic*, meaning 'alive').

The best time to pick the berries is in October when they are coloured but not soft. They make an excellent dark orange jelly which should be eaten with game (traditionally grouse in Scotland), lamb and poultry.

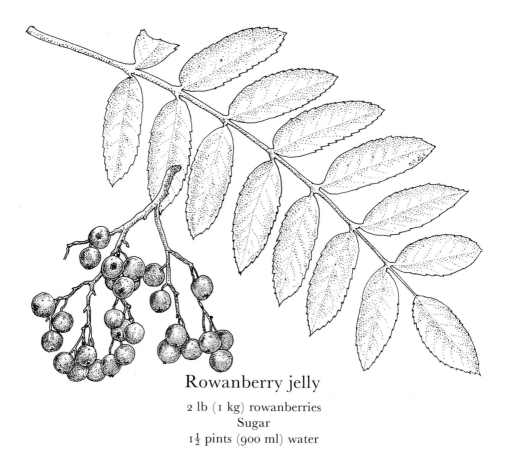

Rowanberry jelly

2 lb (1 kg) rowanberries
Sugar
1½ pints (900 ml) water

Remove the stalks and wash the berries well. Place in a pan with the water and simmer for 45 minutes. Strain through a jelly-bag overnight. Measure the juice and allow 1 lb (500 g) of sugar for each pint of liquid. Bring the liquid back to the boil and stir in the warmed sugar over a low heat. When it is dissolved, boil rapidly until the jelly sets when tested. Skim off any scum and follow the standard procedure.

Rowanberry wine

3 lb (1.5 kg) rowanberries
3 lb (1.5 kg) sugar
½ pint (300 ml) red grape concentrate
2 lemons
7 pints (4 l) water
Yeast and nutrient

Chop the finely peeled rind of the lemons and add to the berries. Pour on the boiling water and leave covered for 3-4 days. Strain onto the sugar and add the concentrate and lemon juice. Stir well to dissolve all the sugar. Allow to cool to room temperature before adding the yeast and nutrient. Cover well and leave in a warm place for 2 weeks. Strain into a fermenting jar and fit an air-lock. Rack when the wine clears and bottle a few months later.

Common Walnut
Juglans regia

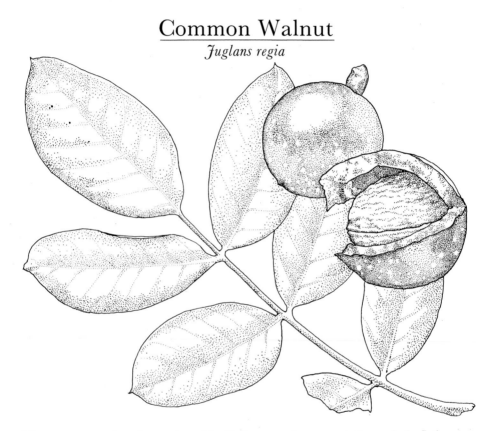

The common walnut is a native of the Balkans, and eastwards through the Lebanon, Iran, Afghanistan, the Himalayas and the Far East. It seems likely that its introduction to Britain was sometime during the middle of the fifteenth century. It is a handsome, fast-growing, deciduous tree reaching heights of 40 to 60 feet (12.25 to 18.5 metres), on occasions much taller. The smooth greyish bark of young trees becomes furrowed longitudinally, and somewhat rugged with maturity. During May and June the large leaves, up to 8 inches long and 4 inches wide (20 and 10 cm), begin to unfurl. The elliptic, almost sessile, leaflets are arranged similarly to those of the common ash, but with only three or four pairs, plus a large terminal leaflet. Both the female flowers and the male catkins appear in May, just before the leaves. The small, green, erect and terminal female flowers occur singly or in small clusters, and on shoots of the year; each have two or three recurvate stigmas. Male catkins are borne on shoots of the previous year's growth, and are very impressive, some 2 to

6 inches (5 to 15 cm) long, cylindrical, green and drooping. The highly esteemed fruit of the walnut ripens during late September and October (except in northern Britain where it only rarely ripens). As the ovary of a fertile female flower expands, so a smooth, green, almost globose, 2-valved drupe is formed, which is about 2 inches (5 cm) in diameter. Eventually the fleshy green outer tissue dries and falls away, to reveal that very familiar wrinkled and fawn-coloured shell of the walnut. Contrary to the common name's suggestion, the tree was never trained to grow against a wall; the derivation comes from the word Wälshnut (Welshnut) meaning 'foreign'. *Juglans* is a contraction of *Jovis glans*—'the nuts of Jupiter'.

Up to 150 lb (70 kg) of walnuts can be gathered from a mature tree annually. They can be picked early in July, whilst they are still green and young for pickling; in this state they contain a large amount of vitamin C. Ripe walnuts, gathered in the autumn, should be kept in their shells for winter use; they keep better if sealed in tight-lidded containers and stored in a dark, dry place.

In the past, oil extracted from walnuts has been used as an edible oil and is still employed in the preparation of artists' paints. Fresh walnuts, when removed from their outer husks, make a good dye. Infusions to be taken internally and externally for the treatment of shingles, sores and swollen glands have been produced from the leaves, fresh or dried.

Walnut marmalade

1 lb (500 g) green walnuts
1¾ pints (1 l) water
1½ lb (750 g) sugar
½ teaspoon lemon juice

Bring the water to the boil. Slice the walnuts thinly and place them immediately into the water so that the colour is preserved. Simmer for 45 minutes until tender. Remove from the heat and stir in the warmed sugar until dissolved. Add the lemon juice and boil the mixture rapidly until it sets when tested.

Walnut fudge

4 oz (100 g) chopped walnuts
1 lb (500 g) sugar
1 tablespoon golden syrup
½ pint (300 ml) double cream or evaporated milk
½ teaspoon vanilla essence

Place the sugar, syrup and cream in a saucepan and bring to the boil, stirring continuously. Simmer for 20 minutes, then add the chopped walnuts and vanilla essence: stir well. Place the pan in cold water and stir quickly until the fudge thickens. Empty into an oiled tin and leave until cold. Cut into squares.

Walnut ketchup

Walnuts (green)
Vinegar
8 oz (250 g) anchovies
2 pints (1200 ml) red wine
2 cloves garlic
1 oz (25 g) each of mace, ginger and pepper

Fill a jar with the walnuts and add sufficient vinegar to cover them. Tie a cover over the jar and leave for a year. Strain off the liquid and put the walnuts on one side. Add all the remaining ingredients to the liquid and boil until the liquid is reduced to half its initial quantity. The following day the ketchup can be bottled. Serve with fish. The walnuts, put on one side, can be used as pickled walnuts.

Walnut bread

4 oz (100 g) shelled walnuts
6 oz (150 g) sugar
1 lb (500 g) flour
2 large teaspoons baking powder
1 small teaspoon salt
1 egg
$\frac{1}{2}$ pint (300 ml) milk

Crush the walnuts with a rolling pin, mix all the ingredients together and leave the mixture to stand for 15 minutes. Put into 2 greased loaf tins. Bake for 45 minutes in a moderate oven (350°F; gas mark 4-5).

Wood Blewit
Lepista nuda (Tricholoma nudum)

Along with the field mushroom (*Agaricus campestris*) and the horse mushroom (*Agaricus arvensis*) the blewits are amongst the few other wild mushrooms that are regularly gathered for eating in Britain. The wood blewit grows quite commonly in woodlands, parklands and gardens, being found singly or in clusters pushing up through a carpet of fallen leaves, or on a heap of compost, and up to 4 inches (10 cm) tall. It can be found from September onwards until the first winter frosts. Young specimens have a convex cap with the margin incurved; this eventually becomes expanded with a central depression. At first the cap is purplish-violet, somewhat darker at the centre, smooth, and $2\frac{1}{4}$ to 4 inches (6 to 10 cm) across. Both the cap and the pale violet gills become brownish-violet with age. The narrow gills are crowded and sinuate; the spores pale pink. The stem is solid and of a mealy texture, sometimes bulbous at base, and violet or greyish-violet with paler silky fibrils. When moist the flesh is bluish-lilac, drying to whitish, and has a pleasantly fruity odour. The blewit or blue leg, *Lepista saeva* (*Tricholoma personatum*), which is usually larger than *L. nuda* but not quite so vividly coloured, and whose gills are never violet, grows gregariously or in rings and is found mainly in grassy pastures.

Both species are good to eat; indeed at one time they were sold in the fruit and vegetable markets in Britain. They have a pleasant smell and their flavour is similar to radishes. Blewits should be gathered on dry days and can be used in similar preparations to mushrooms. Cook them slowly, pouring off the surplus water which they exude freely. Young blewits are delicious fried or grilled.

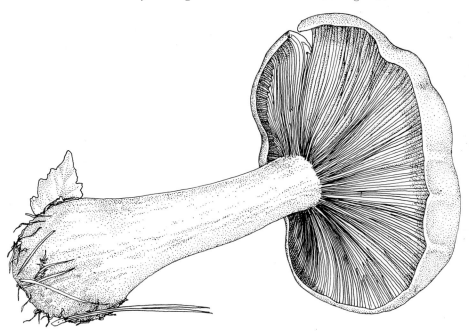

Blewits in white sauce

Blewits
1 onion finely chopped
Chopped parsley
1 oz (25 g) butter
1 oz (25 g) flour
½ pint (300 ml) milk
Salt and pepper

Add a quarter of the milk to the flour, salt and pepper and mix with a wooden spoon to a smooth paste. Bring the remaining milk to the boil, and gradually add to the flour mixture, stirring all the time. Place the sauce on a low heat and stir until it boils; simmer and stir for a further 3 minutes. Slice the blewits and add to the sauce, together with all the remaining ingredients. Cook for a further 10 minutes, stirring continuously.

Jew's Ear Fungus
Hirneola auricula-judae (Auricularia auricula judae)

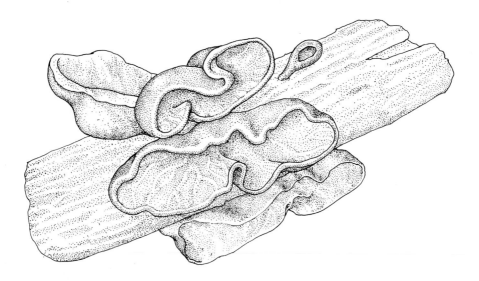

In Britain and Europe the jew's ear fungus occurs mainly on elder trees, growing in tiered groups and firmly attached to branches both living and dead; it may also occur, but only rarely, on other frondose trees including elm, beech, walnut, robinia and willow. It is a common species of up to 3 inches (10 cm) across, typically ear-shaped but often an irregular cup-shape, then flat or saucer-like as it ripens. It is limp, tough, translucent and gelatinous in wet weather, becoming shrivelled and hard during prolonged dry spells. The outer surface is velvety, and varies from dark flesh colour to reddish brown or purplish brown. The inner surface has a spore-bearing layer of tissue (the hymenium), is smooth, shiny, veined and paler than the outer surface. The spores are white. Although it is common throughout the year it is perhaps more so during autumn and early winter. It is a species regularly eaten and much appreciated in the Far East. In China, where a closely related species is culti-vated and grown on cut lengths of oak saplings, it is regarded as a delicacy.

Collect the fungus whilst it is soft, and, although it is edible raw, it is better when cooked. Wash it well, slice and cook for 50 minutes in milk or stock until tender. Serve well-seasoned. It can also be added to stews, casseroles and soups.

Parasol Mushroom
Lepiota procera

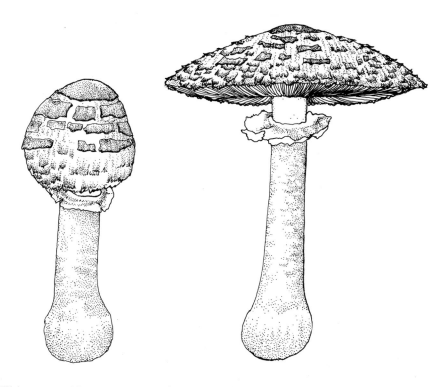

This reasonably common mushroom can be found from July to November but is perhaps most common in the autumn months. It grows in a variety of grassy places such as the margins of frondose woodlands and copses, also in woodland clearings. In young specimens the cap is more or less smooth, practically spherical, and looks something like a short drum-stick; soon expanding to between 4 and 8 inches (10 and 20 cm) across and with a slight but definite umbo. It is greyish-brown in colour with many coarse, dull dark brown, shaggy scales, which also form a marginal fringe. The gills are white and free (not attached to top of stem), and the spores white. The parasol mushroom is one of the largest British species, growing up to 11 inches (27.5 cm) tall. The height of the stem is about twice the diameter of the cap, and is bulbous at the base. At first the stem is brown with a felt-like surface; later it becomes ringed with irregular brown scales, but is always white above the double ring. It separates easily from the cap. The white flesh shows no colour change when cut.

The parasol mushroom is best for eating when picked young and tender, as the flesh tends to become tough with age. Its excellent flavour means that it can be used in the same ways as mushrooms. The caps taste particularly good when fried in hot cooking oil and sprinkled with salt, chives and chopped parsley: the cap-like shape also makes them suitable for stuffing. They can also be dried for use out of season.

Fungi rissoles

1 lb (500 g) fungi (any edible variety)
1 pint (600 ml) vegetable stock
2 eggs
1 onion
Salt, nutmeg, paprika
4 oz (100 g) breadcrumbs

Clean the fungi and place in a pan with the vegetable stock. Boil for 10 minutes, drain through a sieve and chop the cooked fungi finely. Beat the eggs and chop the onion well; add both, together with the salt, nutmeg and paprika, to the fungi. Mix together well and add the breadcrumbs until a firm consistency is achieved. Shape into rissoles and fry quickly on both sides in cooking oil.

Stuffed fungi

8 large fungi caps (e.g. blewits, ceps, milk-caps, parasols)
8 oz (250 g) sausage meat
1 large onion
1 oz (25 g) margarine
2 oz (50 g) breadcrumbs
1 egg
2 tablespoons milk
Salt and pepper
Chopped parsley
1 clove of garlic (crushed)

Chop the onion finely and together with the garlic place in a pan with the margarine: fry gently. Mix the breadcrumbs with the milk and add to the onion. Chop up the stalks of the fungi and mix with the sausagemeat, parsley, salt and pepper, and add to the onion mixture. Bind all the ingredients together with an egg. Stuff the fungi and place on a baking tray in a hot oven (425°F, gas mark 7) for 15 minutes.

Mixed fungi stuffing

8 oz (250 g) mixed edible fungi
2 oz (50 g) margarine
1 tablespoon chopped onion
1 tablespoon chopped parsley
1 tablespoon chopped chives
1 tablespoon lemon juice
3 tablespoons vegetable stock
2 tablespoons flour
Salt and pepper

Melt 1 ounce (25 g) of margarine in a pan and fry the onion, parsley, chives and lemon juice with the stock for 10–15 minutes. Melt the remaining margarine, add the flour and fry until golden brown; season with salt and pepper. Add the diced fungi, mix well and cook for a further 10 minutes. The stuffing is excellent for filling pies, rolls and vegetables.

Mixed fungi soup

1 lb (500 g) mixed edible fungi
2½ pints (1.5 l) vegetable stock
1 oz (25 g) margarine
1 finely chopped onion
1½ tablespoons flour
1 tablespoon chopped parsley
Salt and pepper

Fry the chopped onion in the margarine until golden brown. Cut the fungi into small pieces, add to the onions and continue frying until tender. Sprinkle the flour over the mixture, stir in the vegetable stock and season with salt and pepper. Simmer for half an hour and sprinkle with chopped parsley before serving.

Saffron Milk-cap
Lactarius deliciosus

Coniferous woodlands seem to be the principal habitat of this species, particularly under pines, where it can usually be found from August through to November. The cap varies in diameter from ¾ to 5 in (4 to 12 cm), it is funnel-shaped with an inrolled and occasionally woolly margin; may be viscid or dry. At first reddish-orange with concentric zones of a darker shade, gradually becoming greyish-green with age. The narrow gills are decurrent or adnate, and slightly paler than the cap; later becoming spotted or blotched with green. The stem is shortish, ¾ to 2½ in (2 to 6 cm), may be hollow or stuffed, is concolorous with cap but often slightly pitted, and becomes

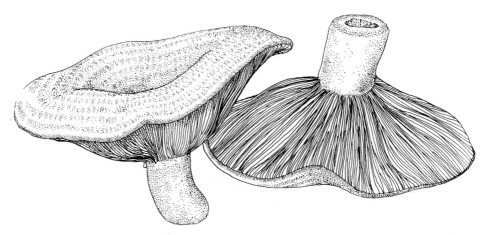

blotched with green particularly if handled. The milk is deep orange red, copious and mild-tasting, gradually turning to greyish-green on exposure to air. The flesh is pinkish to apricot in colour and also turns green with age.

During periods of high humidity *Lactarius deliciosus* is often attacked by the ascomycete *Byssonectria lactaria* when the fruit-body becomes distorted and covered in small pinkish or pinkish-blue excrescences.

For culinary use pick only young specimens and cook and eat as soon as possible. Wash them thoroughly before either grilling or frying in hot butter after first sprinkling with flour and coating with a beaten egg. They should not be stewed, however, because the flavour becomes unpleasant; they are also unsuitable for drying.

Shaggy Cap or Lawyer's Wig
Coprinus comatus

The shaggy cap is a common species which grows well in a loose sandy soil and can be found in meadows, by the roadside, and on rubbish dumps. It seems particularly fond of disturbed ground, and sometimes occurs on newly laid lawns. It reaches heights of up to 10 inches (25 cm), and the cap represents about half the total height. It can be found from May until November in groups or clusters, occasionally singly. When young the white cylindrical cap is narrowest at the base and covered with shaggy, slightly upturned scales. Sometimes a few of the scales are brownish. Later it expands, the margin upturns and splits giving a bell-shaped appearance; the top of the cap is now decidedly brown. At first the thin, broad, white gills are tightly closed like the pages of a book; as the cap expands so the gills become less close and begin to turn pink, later black, and finally they liquefy (this is referred to as auto-digesting). The spores are black. The creamy white stem is smooth, slender, hollow, and erect with a bulbous base; the thin movable ring often slips downwards and finally disappears. The thin watery flesh is white or pinkish.

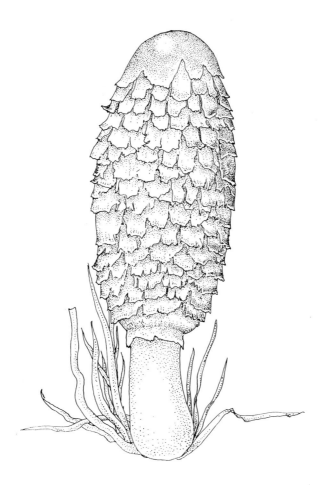

Take only young specimens for the table and eat on the same day; never collect when liquefaction has begun. They have a delicate flavour and are easily digestible. The shape and size of the shaggy cap make it easy to find. To prepare for cooking, first discard the stems and then peel the cap downwards. They are delicious sliced and fried, but can also be stuffed, baked or stewed.

Casseroled Inky (Shaggy) Caps

Young shaggy caps
Cream or top of the milk
Salt and pepper

Prepare the fungi by peeling off the shaggy part of the caps. Place in a casserole dish, cover with the cream and season liberally with salt and pepper. Place in the centre of a moderate oven and cook for $2\frac{1}{2}$ hours.

Laver Seaweed or Purple Laver
Porphyra umbilicalis

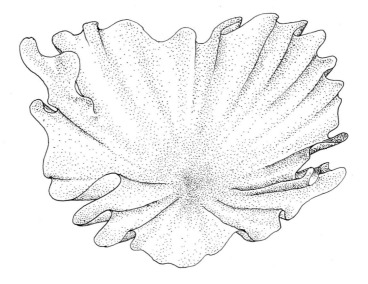

The purple laver seaweed is quite easily identified. It has the same general appearance as the green sea lettuce, but differs in being purplish red or brown, and only green when young. Two other very similar species are found on our shores, *P. laciniata* and *P. vulgaris*. Both are edible but indistinguishable except to the expert. The thin membranous fronds are of irregular shape and wavy, sometimes expanded, at times narrow, and then again often deeply divided into lobes. They are up to 10 inches (25 cm) across, and have a double layer of tissue rather like a deflated balloon. In winter it looks very much like strips that may have been torn from an old black plastic mackintosh. It can be found on exposed beaches in all shore zones, attached by a strong cord of interwoven filaments to stones, shells, rough-surfaced rocks and man-made edifices such as concrete breakwaters and the like; particularly in those areas where the stones are partially or completely covered by sand, giving the impression that the fronds are growing directly from the substrate. When desiccated and bleached after long periods of exposure to the summer sun, it becomes light brown in colour, paper-like and rather brittle, but soon regains its natural texture and colour when covered by the next tide, unless the exposure has been exceptionally prolonged.

Widely distributed, it occurs in Europe, the USA (*P. perforata*), and the British Isles where it is common. In Ireland it is known as 'Sloke', in Scotland 'Slake', and in Devon, England, 'Black Butter'. Seaweeds of the genus *Porphyra* are known as Nori; *P. tenera* and *P. yezoensis*, two cultivated species that are in great demand in Japan, are usually sold in very thin sheets some 8 inches (20 cm) square. Many millions of these are eaten annually by the Japanese.

Purple laver is rich in iodine and the vitamins B and C. It is at its best when collected between late autumn and spring, and for centuries it has been eaten in various ways in Wales, Ireland and western England. It is a particularly popular item of food in South Wales and North Devon, where it is sold prepared for the table. It should be washed well to remove the sand, then boiled in a little water with a few drops of vinegar, until it is soft like well-cooked spinach. The gelatinous mass which results can be mixed with pepper and butter and eaten as a hot vegetable with potatoes and mutton, or served with salad. Once cooked it can be shaped into cakes which are coated with oatmeal or wholemeal flour before being fried. In south Wales, the boiled laver is sold as laver bread. The 'bread' is then fried with bacon or in bacon fat; when it is cooked in this way, the Welsh are particularly fond of their *cig moch a bara lawr*. Its popularity amongst miners is probably due to the fact that it contains essential vitamins and minerals which partly compensate for the deficiencies of life underground.

Laver sauce

2 cups prepared laver
$\frac{1}{2}$ pint (300 ml) milk
1 oz (25 g) butter
1 oz (25 g) flour

Melt the butter and blend in the flour. Gradually add the milk stirring all the time, and when the sauce is smooth and is thickening beat in the laver. This sauce should be served with roast meat, in particular lamb.

Common or Edible Cockle
Cardium edule

It is on open sandy beaches that the cockle is most common, although isolated beds do occur in our polluted estuaries, where along with the mussel it is one of the main filter feeders. Cockles are also found in the brackish waters close to a river mouth, and on occasions even well up the river where the salinity is very low, and here in company with freshwater animals. For some reason the shells are thinner and the ribs fewer in conditions of low salinity. The creamy-coloured shell is familiar to most people, up to $2\frac{1}{2}$ inches (62 mm) long, very globular in shape (more so than other bivalves), and with 24 to 28 radiating ribs that probably help it to grip against the sand. Most of the time is spent shallowly buried beneath the sand; but when the tide comes in it extends two short siphons just above the sand. The lower one permits the entry of water into the gill chamber where microscopic food particles are filtered out through an intricately structured meshwork, and the water subsequently leaves by the upper one. At the ends of the siphons are numerous tentacles on which are borne tiny, 'light and shade' sensitive, eyes; these give warning at the approach of danger. Cockles bury into the sand, and move across it, by virtue of a large and powerful organ, the 'foot', which the animal protrudes specially for this purpose; even in still waters they are capable of moving up to a distance of 39 inches (1 metre) in 24 hours.

Cockles can be collected either by digging, or scraping the sand with a large-toothed rake. They are attacked by starfish, bored into by snails, and at low tide

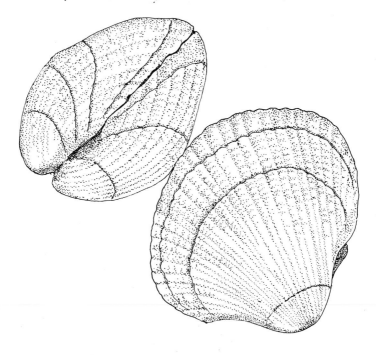

eaten by gulls; but the bird which is partly responsible for its reduced numbers in the Dee and in Morecambe Bay is without doubt the oystercatcher. It has been supposed, but probably overstated, that these birds take more than double the weight of the cockles that are fished commercially; perhaps to credit the oystercatcher with 50 per cent of the total catch would be nearer the mark!

Only the cockles which are intact and more than 1 inch (2.5 cm) wide should be gathered for eating, and are best in winter. After collecting they should not be left in direct sunlight, but, after scrubbing, should be placed in a bucket and covered with clean cold water. When kept in a cool dark place for 8 hours, all the waste sand and grit they contain will be exuded and they will be clean and ready for cooking. To cause the fleshy body to come away from the shell they must first be boiled in a little water or steamed. The cockles should then be removed and are ready for eating; traditionally they are eaten plain, perhaps with a little vinegar (although this tends to destroy the delicious fresh flavour of the cockles). They can be used in place of mussels or oysters and can be fried with bacon or served with salad.

Cockle pie

2 pints (1200 ml) cockles
4 rashers of bacon, roughly chopped
3 tablespoons chopped spring onions or chives
1 cup water
Shortcrust pastry

Line the sides only of a pie dish with thickly rolled pastry. Place the cockles and the water in a pan and cook just long enough for the shells to open. Remove the shells and keep the strained liquid on one side. Put a layer of cockles at the bottom of the dish, sprinkle with some of the chopped spring onions or chives, and add a layer of bacon. Repeat these layers until the dish is full, sprinkle with black pepper and pour over the strained liquid. To complete the pie, criss-cross thin pieces of pastry over the top, and cook slowly until the pastry is baked. The pie is excellent when served hot with new potatoes or cold with a mixed salad.

Cockles and eggs

8 oz (200 g) shelled cockles
2 eggs
1 oz (25 g) bacon fat
Black pepper

Fry the cockles in the bacon fat, stirring and turning continuously. Beat the eggs and pour over the cockles, still stirring the mixture. Season well with black pepper.

Cockle sauce

1 pint (600 ml) cockles
1 oz (25 g) flour
¼ pint (150 ml) milk
2 oz (50 g) butter
Juice of 1 lemon
Pinch of pepper

Place the cockles in a pan without water and heat slowly until they open. Take out the cockles and throw away the shells. Rinse them well before chopping finely. Mix the chopped cockles with the pepper and lemon juice. Melt the butter in a pan and gradually mix in the flour to form a roux. Stir in the milk slowly and cook for 1 minute. Add the cockles and simmer gently for 3 minutes, without the sauce boiling. Serve with white fish.

Common Mussel
Mytilus edulis

The common mussel has a wide distribution, is very common along European coasts, and also inhabits America's north Atlantic shores. Its ability to become established quickly and its density of growth are probably unequalled by any shore animal. Mussels feed on plankton, which they filter from the water by virtue of gills positioned along their entire body length. Each gill has two broad discs comprised of an enormous number of very fine parallel threads. The shell is dark blue and up to 4 inches (10 cm) long; under ideal conditions the growth rate would be about 1 inch (25 mm) annually for the first two or three years, decreasing thereafter. However, living as they do tightly packed on a mussel bed, the growth rate is much reduced and possibly no more than 3 inches (75 mm) over a period of 5 to 7 years; there is no external difference between the sexes. When the shell is opened the animal itself is seen to be dark orange with a white to straw-coloured fringe on the mantle. They attach themselves to rocks by a number of strong silken threads (byssus threads), which are produced by a gland situated in the foot. These extend in all directions, but are mainly directed forward so there is a natural tendency for the mussel to swing round during stormy conditions so that its narrow end heads into the sea. When in dense mussel beds, however, they are so tightly packed that movement is virtually impossible.

Spawning occurs between March and May when females discharge their eggs quite literally by the thousands; it is said that a single female may produce a staggering 25 million in any one season. At the same time the male mussels pour out their milt. The water over the beds soon becomes clouded by the sperm cells, their numbers defying all calculations. Scores of them collect around each single egg, but only one can be successful in gaining entrance. After just a few days tens of thousands of tiny larvae are swimming in the water above the mussel beds; a thin larval shell is soon to form, being quickly replaced by a bivalved version as in the adult. These tiny baby mussels live in countless numbers on the seaweeds of the lower shore, such as the dark brownish-red *Gigartina stellata* which is attached basally to some rock or stone, and known as carragheen moss. Where mussels occur in abundance they form the main food of the dog-whelks. The older shells are bored into, whereas the young mussels are forced apart.

The horse mussel, *Modiolus modiolus*, is distinguished from the common mussel by its larger size (fully grown specimens can be up to 6 inches [15 cm] long), but more easily by the horny fibres that fringe the margin of its very dark shell. The mantle margin, unlike the common mussel, is not fringed. They live off shore, are rarely exposed by very low tides, and occur more abundantly in the north. Specimens found in rock pools, although probably larger than *Mytilus edulis*, are only young ones.

Mussels are in season in autumn and winter and are best eaten on the day they are gathered. They have a delectable flavour but are prone to bacteria and are responsible for many cases of shellfish poisoning. Thus special care must be taken to ensure that the mussels are only gathered at low tides on cleanly washed rocks along the most unpolluted shores. Collect only the large shells and wash thoroughly in several changes of tap water. Scrub the shells and discard any that are open or floating in the water. Leave to stand in cold water for 6 hours before cooking. Remove the beards or tufts of hair which protrude from the mussels with a sharp knife or scissors.

To open the shellfish, place in boiling water, bake in a hot oven or steam. When open, they can be left on half the shell, stuffed with parsley and a little butter, and then grilled. Alternatively, wrap the shelled mussels in thin rashers of bacon, grill and serve with lemon juice. They are also delicious in a soup with onion, garlic and parsley.

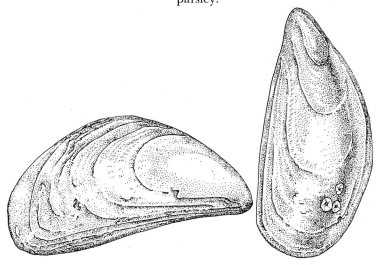

Mussels marinière

2 pints (1200 ml) mussels
2 pieces celery
1 small onion
1 tablespoon tarragon vinegar
1 bunch parsley
2 tablespoons dry white wine
1 pint (600 ml) water
Salt and pepper

Wash the mussels well and remove any that are open. Place all the ingredients in a large pan and heat slowly until the mussels open. In some of them, there may be a small growth which looks like a weed—this should be taken out and the beards removed. Remove half of the shell from each mussel. Bring the liquid back to the boil and strain over the mussels.

Common or Edible Periwinkle
Littorina littorea

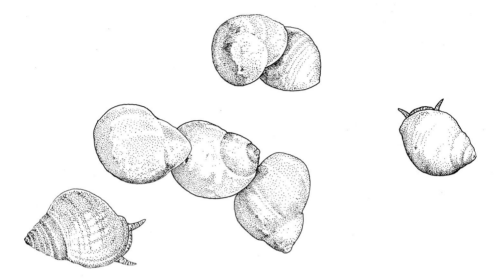

Of the four species of periwinkle that live on the shores of Britain, *L. littorea* is the largest, some $\frac{1}{2}$ to 1 inch (12 to 25 mm) tall. It has a sharply pointed shell, and is usually dark greyish black or red, but always marked with darker concentric lines. It is also the most widespread and the most common, living on bare rocks, amongst stones, and seaweeds, on gravel, even in sand and soft mud. Although often rolled about by stormy seas, it apparently suffers no damage. Just like the mussel and common cockle so the common periwinkle may often be found in the brackish water at the mouth of a river, and at times at some distance up the river where the salinity is quite low and pollution is present. Its foot has a longitudinal cleft so the animal progresses in much the same fashion as man would walk if his ankles were tied together, i.e. by lifting and advancing each half alternately. The diet is herbivorous, food being taken by the rasping action of its lingual ribbon or 'radula' which has a total number of teeth in the region of 3,500.

In the south of England spawning occurs chiefly from roughly February to mid-April. The male impregnates the female, therefore fertilization occurs internally, unlike with the mussels which discharge their eggs and milt for chance fertilization in the sea. The female liberates a gelatinous mass of egg capsules on the surface of seaweed, usually at night-time and on the flood tide. Each capsule contains 3 eggs from which small plankton-feeding larvae will eventually emerge. These become young periwinkles during May and June; and although sexually mature and $\frac{2}{3}$ of an inch (15 mm) high after 18 months, it is not until their third year that they spawn freely. When exposed by the receding tide all species of periwinkle seek the shelter of crevices or seaweed to which they are often found still attached by the foot.

The small periwinkle, *L. neritodes*, is dark-coloured with a bloom such as one would see on sloes, and up to $\frac{1}{5}$ inch (5 mm) high. It lives in the splash zone and may not be wetted during calm weather for days or even weeks on end. Usually most abundant in rock crevices on south facing slopes, it feeds mainly on lichens. Spawning occurs at fortnightly intervals, from September to April, coinciding with the spring tides, the only times when they are completely submerged.

The rough periwinkle, *L. saxatilis (rudis)*, is very variable in colour, ranging from red to black, has 6 to 9 whorls, is $\frac{1}{4}$ to $\frac{1}{2}$ inch (6 to 12 mm) high, and rough to the touch. It is found from upper shore to top of middle shore. The fertilized eggs are completely developed within the female's body, eventually the small shelled young emerge. Characteristic of the species is the rounded opening of the shell.

The flat periwinkle, *L. littoralis (obtusata)*, has even more colour variations, occurring in yellow, orange, red, green, purple, or brown, and occasionally streaked. The shell is sometimes flat-topped, not pointed, is up to $\frac{1}{2}$ inch (12 mm) high, and is found on middle shore and top of lower shore, especially on large seaweeds such as bladderwrack, *Fucus vesiculosus*, and egg or knotted wrack, *Ascophyllum nodosum*, upon which its egg capsules are also deposited; the eggs' greatest danger would seem to be from desiccation rather than from animal predation.

It takes quite a few winkles to make a meal, but it is great fun trying to remove them from their shells. Indeed, it is an art which takes a while to master and involves the skilful removal of their tiny bodies from the safety of their elongated homes. They should first be soaked overnight in clean water, but great care should be taken to cover the container since they are very efficient escapers. To cook, plunge them into boiling slightly salted water and simmer for 10 minutes. Then comes the enjoyable part; first the task of removing them, and secondly the pleasure of eating them, perhaps with a little vinegar and pepper.

Bibliography

Allaby, Michael (and others), *Self-Sufficiency for Everyone*, Macmillan 1975

Altmann, Horst, *Poisonous Plants and Animals*, Chatto & Windus 1979

Beckwith, Lillian, *Lillian Beckwith's Hebridean Cookbook*, Hutchinson 1976

Bryan, John E. and Castle, Coralie, *The Edible Ornamental Garden*, Pitman 1976

'Ceres', *Free for All*, Thorsons Publishers Ltd 1977

Chapman, V. J., *Seaweeds and their Uses*, Methuen (2nd ed.) 1970

Culpeper, Nicholas, *Complete Herbal*, Foulsham 1968

Edlin, H. L., *The Observer's Book of Trees*, Frederic Warne 1975

Eley, Geoffrey, *Wild Fruits and Nuts*, EP Publishing Ltd 1976

Fairhurst, Alan, and Soothill, Eric, *The Blandford Guide to Trees of the British Countryside*, Blandford Press 1981

Fitter, Richard and Alistair, and Blamey, Marjorie, *The Wild Flowers of Britain and Northern Europe*, Collins 1974

Freeman, Bobby, *First Catch your Peacock—A Book of Welsh Food*, Image Imprint 1980

Good Housekeeping Family Library, *Jams and Preserves*, Ebury Press 1973

Hartley, Dorothy, *Food in England*, Macdonald 1954

Hatfield, Audrey Wynne, *How to Enjoy your Weeds*, Frederick Muller Ltd 1969

Hunter, Kathleen, *Health Foods and Herbs*, Collins 1962

Hutchinson, John, *British Wild Flowers* (vols. 1 and 2), David & Charles 1972

Keble-Martin, W., *The Concise British Flora in Colour*, Michael Joseph 1965

Lange, M., and Hora, F. B., *Collins Guide to Mushrooms and Toadstools*, Collins 1963

Loewenfeld, Claire, *Fungi*, Faber 1956

Loewenfeld, Claire, *Nuts*, Faber 1957

Mabey, David and Rose, *Jams, Pickles and Chutneys*, Macmillan 1975

Mabey, Richard, *Food for Free*, Collins 1972

Mabey, Richard, *Plants with a Purpose*, Collins 1977

Masefield, G. B., Wallis, M., Harrison, S. G., Nicholson, B. E., *The Oxford Book of Food Plants*, Oxford University Press 1969

Ministry of Agriculture, *Edible and Poisonous Fungi*, HMSO Bulletin No 43 1947

Ministry of Food, *Hedgerow Harvest*, 1943

O'Céirín, Cyril and Kit, *Wild and Free*, Skilton & Shaw 1980

Patten, Marguerite, *Everyday Cookbook*, Hamlyn 1970

Philips, Roger, *Trees in Britain*, Pan 1978

Polunin, Oleg, *Trees and Bushes of Britain and Europe*, Oxford University Press 1975

Ramsbottom, J., *Edible Fungi*, Penguin 1943

Ramsbottom, J., *Mushrooms and Toadstools*, New Naturalist, 1953

Reekie, Jennie, *Traditional French Cooking*, Macmillan 1975

Soothill, Eric, and Fairhurst, Alan, *The New Field Guide to Fungi*, Michael Joseph 1978

Urquhardt, Judy, *Food from the Wild*, David & Charles 1978

Wakefield, E., *The Observer's Book of Common Fungi*, 1954

Walters, W. D., *Wonderful Herbal Remedies*, Celtic Educational Ltd 1975

Watling, Roy, *Identification of the Larger Fungi*, Hulton 1970

Index

Figures in bold refer to page numbers of colour plates.